Grief *and* Grace

The Sacred Work of Living After Loss

Kate McKay

For permission requests, contact:
Kate McKay
www.katemckay.com

ebook ISBN: 978-1-972014-03-5
Paperback ISBN: 978-1-972014-04-2
Hardback ISBN: 978-1-972014-05-9

Interior design by: Michael Beas

Published by: **Atlas Elite Publishing Partners**

This book is a work of nonfiction. Some names and identifying details have been changed to protect privacy.
Printed in the United States of America

Table of Contents

Dedication

To love, the one thing that grief can never replace.

Letter From My Heart to Yours

Dear Friend,

If this book has found you, my guess is that you're in a season of loss, one that may have cracked you open in ways you didn't expect or ask for.

Maybe your grief is fresh.

Maybe it's something you've carried for years, unsure how to name it.

Wherever you are right now, I want you to know this: you are not alone.

Grief has a way of isolating us, convincing us that no one could possibly understand the shape of our pain. But the truth is, grief is one of the most universal human experiences. It is the price of loving deeply.

Grief is love, interrupted.

And it is also proof that we have cared deeply enough for love to leave its mark.

This book was born from my own encounters with loss, loss that changed me, humbled me, and ultimately taught me something profound about grace.

Along the way I've learned a few things.

Grief doesn't shrink with time, our heart grows around it.

I've learned that tears and laughter can live in the same breath. I've learned that love does not disappear simply because someone we love is no longer physically present.

And perhaps most importantly, I've learned that one of the most powerful ways to honor those we have lost, or the parts of ourselves we have had to leave behind, is to live the qualities we loved most in them.

If they were kind, be kind.

If they were brave, take a risk.

If they were curious, explore something new.

If they loved fully, love again.

That is how love continues.

That is how we become living tributes to what we have loved and lost.

Grief will change you. It cannot help but do that.

But it does not change you only into someone who aches.

It can also make you more gentle.

Wiser.

More awake to what truly matters.

You may begin to see life not as something to rush through or manage, but as something sacred, something to touch, to notice, to receive in ordinary moments that once passed by unnoticed.

As you move through the pages ahead, my hope is that you will find reflection, understanding, and perhaps even moments of comfort.

And when the ache rises, as it will, remember that grace is always near.

It appears in the breath that calms you.

In the friend who calls at the right moment.

In the unexpected strength that returns after you thought it was gone.

Grief may be the place where your story broke open.

But grace is where it continues.

I'm honored to walk this road with you.

With love,

Kate McKay

Author, Coach, and Fellow Traveler in the Landscape of Loss

Poem for the Broken Open

There is a sound
the heart makes when it breaks
quiet at first,
then steady,
like the tide learning its rhythm again.

Grief does not leave;
it lingers,
a shadow of love stretching toward the light.

And one day,
without warning,
grace appears,
not to take the pain,
but to teach us
how to live inside it
and still
to choose love.

Author's Note

For Anyone Who Has Ever Lost Something They Loved

This book is for anyone who has experienced grief in any form: the loss of a person, a relationship, a dream, a marriage, a pet, a home, a season of life, or even the version of yourself you once knew.

Because, despite what we may automatically think of when we hear the word, *grief* is not reserved for death alone.

It is the ache that rises when something we've loved changes form, when what once gave us belonging, meaning, or safety is no longer within our grasp.

Every grief carries meaning because where there is grief, there was love.

And love, even when transformed by loss, still has the power to shape and redeem us. This truth is why I wrote this book.

This book, *Grief and Grace,* is an invitation to not rush your healing or somehow magically make sense of your pain, *but to honor it.* To allow it to teach you, perhaps even to soften you: to reveal what remains.

You may find your own story in these pages: heartbreak, confusion, courage, surrender, even laughter that feels like defiance. I hope that as you read, you'll feel less alone in your journey and more at home in your own fragile, yet resilient humanity.

Grief and grace are not opposites. They are companions: two sides of the same coin, teaching us how to live with an open heart, even after it's been broken to pieces. And in that tender space where grief and grace meet, may you come to see that the love was never lost, it's simply changing form.

Introduction

When the Heart Breaks Open

There is no way to prepare yourself for the moment your child dies.

Even now, years later, I can still feel the ache when I say his name out loud. The world didn't just lose a beautiful soul that day; I lost a piece of my identity as a mother: my compass, my mirror, my boy. On October 14, 2017, the ground dropped out from under me, and I remember thinking, *How do I go on from here? How does a life keep moving when its center is gone?*

Grief, I've learned, doesn't just visit you; it moves in. It settles into your chest, your breath, your nervous system. It changes how you experience sound, light, and time. Laughter feels too loud. Morning light feels intrusive, almost cruel. Food tastes different. Sleep becomes unfamiliar. Your whole system remembers what happened long before your thoughts can make sense of it.

Grief reaches us at the most primal level. It doesn't ask permission. It doesn't care how capable, strong, or prepared you thought you were. It dismantles the assumptions you lived by and leaves you standing in a world that no longer follows the rules you understood.

In the beginning, there is no meaning to make, only shock, loss, and survival. Only the question every grieving person eventually asks: *Who am I now?*

This book is not about getting over loss. It is about learning how to live after it. It is about what happens when grief cracks you open and refuses to let you go back to who you were before. It is about grace, not as something tidy or neatly packaged, but as the quiet, persistent presence that meets us in the aftermath and helps us keep going when we don't know how.

Grief and Grace is for those who have lost someone they love and feel forever changed. It is for those who carry sorrow in their bodies and questions in their hearts. It is for those who are still standing, even when standing feels like the only thing they can manage.

If you are here, you are not broken.
You are human.
And you are not alone.

When Will first died, I tried to manage it the best I could. I had two other kids to care for, a business to run. I thought I could outwork grief, outlift it, outrun it. That's what strong people do, right? We keep moving.

But grief, that sneaky old fellow, has its own way of finding you.

I remember one morning, not long after Will died. I had just woken up, lying next to my daughter Sophie. We had been sleeping together in those early days, holding on to each other, not wanting to face the terror alone. The morning sun stretched gently across her face, and for a fleeting second, everything felt suspended … still, and almost (dare I say) peaceful.

And then the gut-punch of truth came rushing in: Will was gone. He wasn't coming back. The massive ache of it tore through my chest, hollowing me out from the inside. Slow tears tumbled down my cheeks, and yet somehow, those tears were different. I was different. For a brief moment, I felt acceptance; grace swooped in at that moment with gentleness that held my breath, questioning if the feeling was real.

And as those tears fell, I felt my soul open. Acceptance mixed with confusion, sorrow intertwined with surrender. I didn't know who I was anymore or what my life would even look like moving forward. But I sensed at that moment that there existed, somewhere within me, a mustard seed of faith that I was going to somehow, some way make it through this horrific loss.

Grief rips us to our core. It shatters the illusion that we're in control and leaves us face-to-face with the unbearable truth of how much a single life, an experience, can matter to us. And yet, on that morning, I felt something else too: something quiet and inexplicable. Grace. It swept in softly, not to erase the pain, but to sit beside it. It whispered what I couldn't yet say aloud: "Hey Kate, your love for Will doesn't end here."

I know now that love just changes form: into presence, into memory, into the unseen ways we stay connected to those who shaped us, through may I even be bold enough to say, through eternity.

That morning was the moment I began to understand: we don't get over grief. We grow through it if we are willing, even for one breath, that the love is still here.

Grief doesn't make us less whole: it simply reveals how vast our hearts really are. It exposes the parts of us we didn't know could bear so much, and somehow, it teaches us to love again, not despite the pain, but through it.

The purpose of this book isn't to fix grief or offer tidy steps toward closure. (Truth Drop: closure is a myth) It's about honoring what's been lost, learning from what remains, and allowing something sacred to grow in the cracks that grief leaves behind.

Grief and grace: two sides of the same coin.
Pain and presence.
Loss and love.
They walk together, sometimes haltingly, but always truthfully.

I hope that through these pages, you'll find your own sense of self again, one that holds both the ache and the awe of being alive and honoring the love that remains deep within us.

Welcome to a place where grief and grace can coexist, and where your new self is born anew, messy, befuddled, maybe, and yet still here to honor and live into what was

Chapter 1

The Many Faces of Grief

We tend to think of grief as one thing: the deep ache that follows death or loss. But grief is far more complicated than that. It's not just about losing a person or losing our sense of identity. It's about losing a version of ourselves we thought we'd always have.

It's the marriage that ended. The friendship that faded. The dream that didn't happen. The pet that died. The good health that changed. The faith that cracked.

Grief shows up wherever love or attachment has lived: it's the dark shadow of our connection that no longer is there. And because our human connection takes many forms, so does our grief.

Some losses are visible and honored. Others are invisible, private, and hard to explain.

There's the obvious heartbreak of death. But there's also the quiet mourning of seasons that end, children growing up, careers shifting, identities changing.

You may find yourself in one of these forms of grief, or in several. Let that be okay. Grief rarely fits in just one category. (We will expand on these different forms of grief in a later chapter.)

There's **anticipatory grief**, feeling the loss before it even happens.
And **functional grief**, when we keep going, smiling, doing all the things, while something inside us quietly aches.
There's **ambiguous grief**, when someone is still here, but the relationship or the version of them you loved is gone.
There's **disenfranchised grief**, the losses society doesn't acknowledge, but your heart can't ignore.
There's **identity grief**, mourning the person you were before life changed everything.
There's **secondary grief**, the cascade of smaller losses that follow the big one, shifting routines, dreams, and the future you thought you'd have.
There's **delayed grief**, when the emotions arrive long after the world thinks you should be "better."
And there's **compounded grief**, when losses layer on top of each other, and you're grieving more than one thing at the same time, even if no one else can see it.

If one of these hits home, you're not imagining it, exaggerating it, or "making it a big deal." Your grief has a name, and naming it is the first step towards healing.

We live in a culture that wants us to "get over it," tidy it up, and move on. But grief doesn't work that way. It doesn't follow a timeline or an agenda. It's not linear: it loops, circles, ebbs, and flows.

I remember thinking, early on after my son Will died, *I'll be better by the one-year mark.*
But grief had other plans.

It came in waves: unexpected, inconvenient, uncontrollable.
Sometimes it showed up as tears.
Sometimes, as anger.
Sometimes, as exhaustion.
And sometimes, as that hollow stillness where I'd just stare into space, too weary to care.

Kate McKay

For a long time, I thought something was wrong with me; that I wasn't "doing grief right."
People treated me differently. And I now know why… I *was* different. Grief rearranges you, sometimes so profoundly that the world doesn't quite know what to do with the version of you that comes after loss.

People's responses to your grief will vary as much as the types of grief we experience: kindness and impatience, compassion and indifference.
Some will want to hold you.
Some will pull away.
Some will lean in closer because your pain mirrors something in them.
These occurrences add another layer of complexity to grief. We stumble through all of it, the hurt itself, and the reactions to the hurt, trying to make sense of a world that no longer fits.

But even here, there is truth:
There is no right way.
There's only your way.

Grief is not a skill to master or a milestone to hit. It's a terrain you learn as you walk it: uneven, surprising, alive. And grace is what meets you along the way: in the breath you didn't know you needed, the person who shows up when you least expect it, the moment your heart softens even though it still hurts like hell.

If you're somewhere in this landscape, raw, unsure, overwhelmed, numb, you're not behind.
You're not failing.
You're not lost.

You're human.
And you're healing, even when it doesn't look like it.

During this time is where you may start to see grief for what it really is: not a puzzle to fix or a season you "get over," but a companion, whether we want it or not, that walks beside you as you grow into someone new.

Reflection Questions

1. Which type of grief resonated with you the most, and what about it felt familiar in your body or your story?

2. How has grief changed the way you see yourself: your identity, your relationships, even the world around you?

3. Where in your life do you feel the need to "do grief right," and what might it look like to give yourself permission to grieve in your own way?

Chapter 2

The Myth of Being Strong

We live in a world that rewards a very specific kind of strength, and it isn't always a healthy one.
It praises grit and endurance, the kind that keeps going at all costs, holds everything together, and never lets the cracks show.

The message is clear:
Be strong.
Don't burden anyone.
Don't talk about anything that will make someone else uncomfortable.

But grief doesn't honor those rules.

It doesn't care about appearances or performance. It slips through the seams of even the strongest façade and whispers, *"You're human. You're hurting. And you don't have to pretend."*

Apparently, I missed that memo. I was given a different lesson long before the grief of losing my son arrived.

Because the strategies we develop as children to survive don't disappear when we grow up. They become our blueprint. They become our wiring. And while people respond to childhood trauma in a thousand different ways, this was my way:

Keep moving.
Stay cheerful.
Stay prepared.
Don't get stuck anywhere long enough for anything to swallow you.

I learned to read a room before I learned to read myself. I was a hypersensitive kid: every rejection, every shift in tone, every sigh or slammed door felt personal. I cried easily. I was an easy target for my siblings' teasing because nothing bounced off me. I absorbed it all. And in a chaotic environment, that hypersensitivity turned into hypervigilance. I stayed alert, scanning for cues, trying to avoid the next emotional blow.

Staying in motion became my protection.
Positivity became my cover.

I tried to lift my mother's spirit where I could with my silliness, my expressiveness, and my affectionate nature. She carried so much: nine children, depression, exhaustion, a house that seemed always on the edge of chaos. When my siblings acted out, I instinctively tried to entertain my mom, because I could sense the heaviness pressing on her.

My technique was successful for many years, imprinting in my soul the belief that to survive in the world, I must adapt and try to buffer others from suffering. Staying upbeat was my armor. It kept me from sinking into the chaos around me. Being still, emotionally or physically, never worked for me. It made me feel trapped, unsafe. I needed to be taking action to feel free.

And as I grew older, my outer world reinforced the same lessons my childhood had already taught me:

Stay positive.
Don't drag anyone down with your troubles.
Keep going.
Be self-reliant.
Handle it yourself.

So I did. And I got really good at it.

In fact, movement directly correlated to my success. Professionally, I built, hustled, acted fast, and made things happen. Athletically, I pushed, trained, competed, using my body to burn through what my heart wasn't ready to feel. Intellectually, I stayed curious, engaged, and always expanding. Romantically, I kept busy dating men drawn to my chaos and charm, but they didn't offer safety, which was an illusion to me anyway.

Movement served me.
It shaped me.
It kept me alive.

But it also cost me something.

All that motion, all that hypervigilance, stunted my ability to build safety in relationships.
I didn't know how to rest inside another person.
I didn't know how to trust stillness or closeness.
I didn't know how to let myself need anything.

When people misunderstood me, my intensity, my expressiveness, and my emotional depth, I felt the rejection deeply. But I kept going. I'd learned early that being misunderstood was the norm, and depending on anyone else was out of the question.

So when grief finally arrived years later, real, devastating grief, it exposed everything I had never learned: I had mastered endurance, not rest.
Success, not openness.
Self-protection, not trust.

I didn't know how to fall apart safely.
I only knew how to keep moving because motion had always been my safety.

And layered underneath that was my ADHD wiring:

The constant intensity.
The emotional sensitivity.
The feeling of never quite fitting in.

In a big family where noise and disorder were normal, my internal world felt even louder. I was the happy, upbeat one on the outside, but inside I carried this deep, unspoken ache: Where do I belong? Who am I safe with?

Early trauma shaped all of that. It made me alert, hyper-responsible, emotional, and constantly scanning for cues.

And then there was Matt. My brother. We were born only eighteen months apart.

In a family as big as ours, children get paired, almost like little sub-teams inside the chaos. And for us, it was always Kate and Matt. Two kids tethered together, bombing through the neighborhood, swinging from trees, splitting chores, and navigating through the same family storms.

He was my closest companion.
The one who understood our family's chaos without explanation.
The one whose presence made instability survivable.

Losing him wasn't just losing a sibling. It was losing my other half. So when Matt was murdered in 1987, everything in me shattered. I went into survival mode.

My own grief didn't matter, or I convinced myself it didn't. My parents were shattered. My family was breaking up. And so I jumped into the role that eventually became my superpower:

Do the next thing.
Stay responsible.
Stay useful.
Stay small.
Stay alert.

Sibling loss is often dismissed or minimized, but it is profound. It rearranges your internal map. And because the world rarely acknowledges it, you carry invisible grief while everything around you falls apart.

Kate McKay

Growing up in a family of eleven, chaos was constant: addiction, rage, depression, instability, sudden moves. Safety wasn't a given. Trust arrived inconsistently.

I learned early that the only thing I could control was myself: my behavior, my movement, my emotional containment.
So I became a moving target.

If I stayed still, I risked being swallowed by everything I didn't yet have words for.

So when Matt died, I didn't fall apart, at least in public.
I didn't scream or collapse.
I calculated.
I assessed.
I stayed in action; the only strategy I had ever known.

And decades later, when my son Will died by suicide in 2017, I did the same thing.

I stayed in motion.
I organized.
I handled it.

While everyone seemed to be falling apart, I made the calls, arranged the services, delivered the eulogy, and held others through their tears while mine stayed locked inside.

People saw composure, capability, steadiness, but none of that was calm. It was control.
And control was the only safety I had ever trusted. Because if I weren't in control, I would feel lost. Control felt like my sacred responsibility- my role in the chaos.

What no one could see was the ocean underneath: decades of postponed grief, stacked trauma, childhood wounds, the loss of my brother, the loss of my son, the feeling of being different, the emotional wiring that made everything more intense.

None of it had disappeared.

It had simply waited.
All grief does.
And eventually, it rises.

At first, I thought my ability to keep it together meant I was healing well. I was what some call a "practical griever:" the one who gets things done, manages the details, performs the tasks, stays functional.

Now I know it was simply my body and spirit doing what they had always done: Protecting me until I had the strength to truly feel it.

Delayed grief wasn't failure.
It was wisdom.
It was my system saying:
"Not yet. You still have to keep it together."

And when the time finally came to stop managing and start mourning, it was brutal, but it was also the beginning of what I now understand as true strength. The kind that comes not from control but from *surrender.* From letting myself be seen.

I used to think breaking down meant weakness.
Now I know it was the bravest thing I've ever done.

Because there is no one right way to grieve.

Some cry.
Some go silent.
Some get angry.
Some clean, organize, or work harder.
Some escape into service or distraction.
Some, like me, stay in motion until stillness finally finds them and cracks them open.

Grief wears many faces, and each one deserves compassion.

Kate McKay

I'm grateful now for the girl and the woman who held it all together.
She got me through the impossible.
But I am equally grateful for the woman who finally allowed herself to fall apart.

Both are me.
Both are strong.
Both were necessary.

Professional support, safe people, movement, faith, reflection: these have been acts of fierce self-respect. They've helped me learn to live through my trauma, not around it.

Strength isn't pretending everything's fine.
It's staying present long enough to let love reach the places that still hurt.

Reflection Questions

1. What did "being strong" mean in your family growing up, and how does that show up in the way you grieve now? Were emotions welcomed, managed, hidden, or dismissed?

2. When have you relied on control, busyness, or competence to get through pain, and what happened when you finally allowed yourself to feel instead of manage?

3. Which version of you deserves more compassion right now, the one who held everything together, or the one who finally let herself fall apart? What would it look like to honor both?

Chapter 3

Guilt, Shame, and the Courage to Tell the Truth

Today, as a coach and grief educator, I walk beside others as they learn to trust the same messy, sacred process I've come to know myself. I remind them often: grief is not a detour from life. It is part of the path toward becoming whole.

And almost always, grief brings companions.

Guilt.
Shame.

They arrive quietly and linger loudly. We replay what we should have known, what we should have said, what we should have prevented. We tell ourselves we failed the people we loved. Or that we've failed ourselves for not healing faster, cleaner, or more gracefully.

Guilt and shame are closed rooms.

They trap us.
They keep the air from moving.
They convince us that silence is safer than truth.

But silence doesn't heal. It suffocates.

Speaking our truth, no matter how painful, unpolished, or frightening, opens a window. It lets air back into the room. It allows light to enter where everything has gone stale and dark.

When we name what hurts, when we cry without apology, when we allow someone to witness our humanity without rushing us or trying to fix us, healing begins to move again.

In my work, I remind clients that transformation isn't about repairing what's broken. Grief is not a problem to solve. It's an experience to honor.

Healing comes from telling the truth about what happened, feeling what demands to be felt, and allowing new meaning to rise slowly, steadily from the ashes.

I hold space in many ways. Sometimes in silence. Sometimes through movement. Sometimes through prayer. Sometimes, through laughter in the middle of the hardest times, because every person's healing shows up differently, and all of it is worthy of respect.

The greatest gift we can offer one another is permission.

Permission to be exactly where we are.
Permission to sit beside someone in sorrow without trying to tidy it up.
Permission to believe that even in the darkest places, something sacred is still unfolding.

Grief may be the wound, but grace is the light that seeps through the cracks, if we are brave enough to let it in.

You don't have to fix the pain to honor it. You only have to stay in your truth and remain open long enough for the light to do what light always does: Find its way in.

Reflection Questions

1. Where in your own process do guilt or shame still whisper to you?

2. What would it look like to speak your truth, without editing it, to someone you trust or even to the page?

3. How might you offer someone else grace today simply by listening without trying to fix it?

Chapter 4

When the Heart Breaks Open

There are times in life when the bottom drops out, and nothing feels safe anymore. The world keeps going. People keep showing up, making plans, living their lives. But inside, something fundamental has broken, and you know, without needing words, that you are not the same person you were before.

Your body reacts first. Your breath goes shallow. Your chest tightens. Your nervous system goes on high alert. You're still standing, but whatever was holding you together has cracked, and no amount of willpower is going to fix it.

This kind of breaking isn't dramatic. It's brutal in a quieter way. It happens internally. A collapse you carry inside your own skin. One minute you're functioning. Next, you're staring at the wreckage of your own life, trying to understand how everyone else keeps going while you're barely upright.

Grief hits like a bomb going off at the center of your life. There's no warning. No time to brace. One second, life is familiar enough to manage, and the next, everything detonates. And when the dust settles, the landscape is unrecognizable.

What was once solid is gone.
What was once covered is exposed.
What you relied on, believed in, or counted on no longer exists the way it did before.

Grief doesn't just destroy, it reveals. It strips away what was fragile but hidden. It exposes fault lines you didn't know were there. You're left standing in open terrain with no shelter, no clear direction, and no easy answers.

And here's the part people don't like to admit:

Grief is no joke.

It doesn't hand out lessons on a timeline. It breaks things. It humbles you. It asks more of you than you think you have.

This is where grief actually begins. Not in the tears or the rituals or the words people offer, but in the moment when control is gone and pretending stops working.

Grief doesn't ask what you're ready to face. It just uncovers what's been waiting.

And if we're being real?
Grief feels a lot like playing a twisted version of the game *Candy Land.*

Do you remember that game? We all played it, thinking the whole point was to get to the Candy Castle: our little kid version of "heaven on earth." And even then, there was this bittersweet truth baked into it: you never knew what the next card would bring. That was the excitement. You'd pull a card hoping for a big move, and sometimes you got it. Other times, you got sent straight to the Molasses Swamp with Gloppy, totally stuck and frustrated.

And then there were the amazing card pulls: Princess Lolly, or pulling a card that skipped you way ahead, that feeling of *Yes, finally.*
That rush? That tiny hit of hope? We lived for that as kids.

Looking back now, that game was more real-life than I ever realized. We thought we were just playing a board game with friends, but we were actually practicing for life: the highs, the setbacks, the sweetness, the slowdowns, and the not-so-fun surprises. Life isn't straight, predictable, or fair. Neither was the game. But both taught us the same thing: the next card might change everything.

You think you're making progress.
You believe you're finally getting somewhere.
And then, bam, you pull a card that sends you straight back to the beginning.

No warning.
No logic.
No fairness.

Just the sinking feeling of,
Oh no … not again.

One day, you wake up feeling strangely okay, almost hopeful.
And the very next day, you're knocked down again, like you're wading through emotional quicksand, wondering how you ended up back in the pain you thought had loosened its grip, even just a little bit. That's grief. One minute, the sky feels open, the next you're right back in a blinding rainstorm, trying to figure out which way is forward.

And the truth is, most of us learn how to handle pain long before we ever face real loss. We copy what we saw growing up. In my family, grief didn't speak; it buzzed under the surface. It showed up as agitation, tension, that subtle charge in the air that made me feel like I had to stay on alert. I learned to read the room before anyone said a word. So I found my peace outside: running through the woods, lying in the grass, climbing trees, or burying myself in a book. Nature and stories were the only places where my nervous system stopped buzzing.

So when loss hit my life, I didn't have a model for healing. I just knew how to survive. Keep going. One breath. One shaky step. Do what you can to stay upright while everything inside you is rearranging itself without your permission.

Grief isn't something you conquer.
It isn't something you master.

You don't move *on*, you move *with*.
And it changes you whether you agree to it or not.

Because grief isn't the end of love.
It's love in its rawest form, stripped of anything that used to make sense.

And when your heart breaks wide open, you start to realize grief isn't an enemy. It's a companion. A demanding one. A relentless one. But also a wise one. It walks with you through the wreckage after the grief bomb goes off, helping you see what's been buried and what's been exposed.

The breaking isn't the ending.
It's the beginning of the person you're becoming next.

Grief is not the end of love.
Grief is the form love takes when everything else falls away.

And when your heart breaks open, truly open, you begin to understand grief not as an enemy to defeat, but as a companion. An unpredictable, demanding, exhausting companion. But a wise one.

Because the breaking is not the end. It is the beginning of becoming someone new.

Chapter 5

Our Changing Relationship with Grief and Loss

If you've made it this far, it's because grief has touched your life in some way, and because part of you still wants to live well.

That matters.

For most of human history, death wasn't hidden. People died at home, surrounded by familiar hands and familiar voices. Grief had witnesses. Mourning had rituals. There were casseroles, candles, wakes, funerals, and neighbors who didn't need the right words: friends, even strangers, just showed up.

Those rituals didn't fix anything.
But they said something essential to the grieving:

You're not alone.
We'll carry this with you.

Grief had somewhere to go.

As medicine advanced and life expectancy grew, death slowly moved out of the home and into hospitals. Behind curtains. Into quiet rooms. Into the care of professionals.

And grief followed.

Quietly.
Privately.
Often invisibly.

We softened the language. *Passed away, gone to a "better place."* We stopped talking about death at the dinner table. We expected people to return to work after a few days. We praised strength. We rewarded productivity. We told people to move on, sometimes gently, sometimes not at all.

By the mid-20th century, we had become deeply uncomfortable with grief. We wanted things tidy and predictable. Grief, messy, nonlinear, inconvenient, didn't cooperate.

So it didn't disappear.

It went underground.

Into bedrooms.
Into marriages.
Into bodies.
Into silence.

And then slowly, something changed.

The Courage to Name the Unspoken

That change began with Elisabeth Kübler-Ross.

Before she became known for her work on death and dying, she was a little girl in Switzerland, one of identical triplets. She once shared an experience that stayed with her forever. Sitting on her father's lap, he asked:

"Which one are you?"

However he meant it, the question landed deeply.

It sparked a vow that would shape her life:

Everyone deserves to be seen.
Every story matters.
No one is interchangeable.

That vow followed her into hospitals, into rooms where people were dying, into conversations no one else wanted to have. She sat with fear. With regret. With longing. With wisdom. She listened when others turned away.

In 1969, she published *On Death and Dying*, giving language to what had been carried in silence for generations: **denial, anger, bargaining, depression, acceptance**.

Not as rules.
Not as steps.
But as words, finally, for the chaos.

Later, her student, and my mentor, David Kessler, expanded that work by naming what so many people were already reaching for: meaning.

Meaning wasn't a way out of grief.
It was a way to live with it.

Together, they made grief speakable.
They gave it dignity.
And they opened a door the rest of us could walk through.

From Understanding Grief to Living with It

Still, if you've ever thought, "*Why does this grief keep coming back?,*" you're not alone.

Grief isn't something you pass through and leave behind.
It's something you learn how to live with.

That's why psychologist William Worden's Tasks of Mourning resonated so profoundly with me.

Worden didn't frame grief as a series of stages to "complete" or boxes to check. Instead, he understood grief as *work*; work we return to again and again, over a lifetime, as love and loss continue to shape us.

His model names four essential tasks:

1. Accepting what is real.
2. Feeling what hurts.
3. Adjusting to a world that has changed.
4. And finding ways to carry love forward.

Not in order.
Not on a timeline.
Not once and done.

Just honestly.

Some days we may find ourselves accepting the reality of loss, only to circle back, years later, to another level of pain we didn't know was still there. Other days, we may experience genuine peace, only to be surprised by grief when the world reminds us of what's missing.

This doesn't mean we're failing.
It means we're human.

What I appreciate most about Worden's work is the permission it offers. Permission to revisit these tasks without shame. Permission to understand that grief is not linear, and healing is not a finish line we cross.

And even then, no single model tells the whole story.

Grief is too personal, too relational, too sacred to be fully contained by any framework. Models can guide us, but they cannot capture the way loss reshapes identity, faith, purpose, or the way love continues long after someone is gone.

That's why I see Worden's tasks not as instructions, but as companions, and markers along the path that remind us we're not lost, even when the terrain keeps changing.

Grief asks us to do this work not to "get over" what we've lost, but to learn how to live honestly in a world forever altered by love.

And that work unfolds in its own time.

The Grief & Grace Integration Framework™

This framework exists because grief needs more than one lens. Personally, I need a visual cue to assimilate a concept so that I can in some way understand it

Some models help us name what we're feeling.
Some help us engage in the work.
Some help us remember that love doesn't end.

And some bring us back into the present moment, where grief and grace actually live.

The *Grief & Grace Integration Framework*™ brings these together:

- **Naming the experience** so you know you're not broken
- **Engaging the work** so you're not stuck waiting to feel better
- **Finding meaning** so love can keep shaping your life
- **Present-moment connection** so grief isn't abstract, but lived

At the center is what I call **Grace in Action**.

Not grace as an idea, but as something that is living and breathing.

What Integration Looks Like In Real Life

One client came to me years after a loss, worn down and frustrated with herself. Certain memories still took her breath away, and she believed that meant she was failing.

She said, "I thought I'd be past this by now."

I asked her with a caring, gentle smile, "Hmm, who told you that?"

That question changed the tone of everything.

As we talked, it became clear she had learned how to function, but not how to breathe, to heal, or evolve within the life she was living. She had accepted what happened and adjusted her routines, but she hadn't permitted herself to feel what still surfaced.

I asked, **"What happens in your body when the wave hits?"**
And later, **"What are you saying to yourself at that moment?"**

What shifted wasn't her grief.
It was her *relationship* with it.

She stopped judging herself, and meaning began to emerge quietly, naturally, without pressure. My client started to feel the grip of grief loosen. She began to truly feel a sense of peace within that she thought she had forever lost.

You deserve that sense of peace, too.

Another Way Integration Shows Up

Another client avoided speaking about his deceased wife altogether. He thought staying composed was respectful. When it felt appropriate, I asked gently:

"Tell me about her."
"What did you love most?"

He paused, let out a big sigh and then laughed out loud and said, "Grief sucks," and we both cracked up.

I then asked, **"Where do you feel them when you say her name?"**
And later, **"What part of who you are today came from loving her?"**

In that moment, grief and love sat side by side.

He didn't fall apart, get angry, or close down. He opened up, softened, breathed, and remembered: the joy and sorrow. He remembered the love.

Finding Meaning: How Love Continues

Meaning isn't closure.

It's how love keeps going.

It shows up as:

- Continuing the bond
- Honoring the legacy
- Integrating the lesson

Meaning doesn't erase grief.
It gives it a place in your life that doesn't consume you.

Grace in Action

Grief isn't something to solve.

It's something to tend.

Grace lives in motion; in showing up, in staying present, in choosing to live forward without leaving love behind.

That's the work.
And that's the invitation.

Reflections

1. What truth about my grief am I ready to name honestly, without fixing it?

2. How is love still shaping who I'm becoming?

3. What does living forward with intention look like right now, today, not someday?

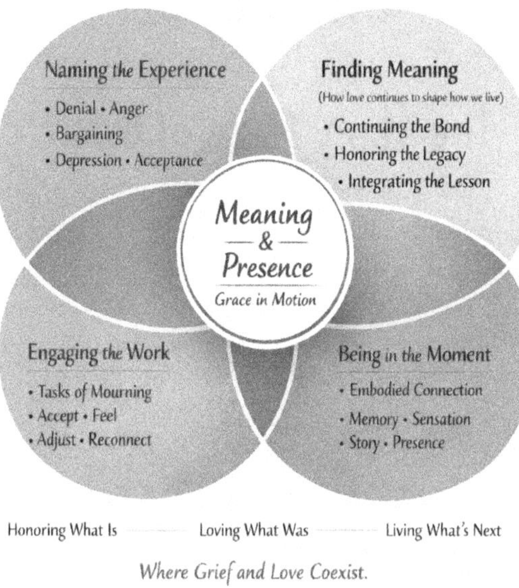

Book a Discovery Call with Kate https://calendly.com/katemckay/restorative-coaching

Chapter 6

The Many Faces of Grief

Grief is not reserved for funerals.
Grief is love meeting change.

Here are the deeper layers of grief we experience across the human journey:

1. Death-Related Grief

Losing someone to death is a loss everyone recognizes. It is the empty chair, the silence in the kitchen, the moment you reach for the phone to call someone who is no longer alive. It asks impossible questions: *Who am I without them? Does life still hold meaning?*

Example:
A mother still sets a place for her son at Thanksgiving three years after he died. Her hands know the ritual even when her intellectual mind tells her to stop.

2. Relationship Grief

The grief of breakups, divorces, estrangement, separations. We grieve not just the person, but the routines, the safety, the identity, and the future we imagined.

Example:
Sandra, my client, wasn't grieving the man she divorced as much as the life they had built: coffee rituals, laughter, predictable comfort, the sense that tomorrow had certainty.

3. Identity Grief

This is the grief of becoming someone new before you're ready, through menopause, aging, trauma, illness, career upheaval, or parenting shifts. Identity grief whispers, *I don't know who I am anymore.*

Example:
A woman whose children leave for college sits in her quiet kitchen and doesn't recognize her own life.

4. Loss of Dreams & Expectations

This grief arises when the imagined future dissolves: the baby that never came, the marriage you hoped would heal, the career that collapsed. You mourn not only what happened, but what *didn't.*

Example:
An entrepreneur closes her business after years of sacrifice and feels like she is burying a part of her soul.

5. Invisible & Unacknowledged Grief

These are the losses no one talks about: aging, friendships fading, pets dying, losing community or belonging. These griefs often hurt the most because you feel them alone.

Example:
A man cries in his car when his dog dies, ashamed to tell his friends because he thinks it "shouldn't matter this much."

6. Faith & Meaning Grief

Losing a sense of spiritual faith fills us with a deep emptiness: the loss of certainty, the collapse of old beliefs, the feeling that God has gone silent. We feel disoriented, lonely.

Example:
A woman prays after her husband dies and feels nothing. She wonders if God has abandoned her, and her heart is filled with guilt and shame.

7. Anticipatory Grief

Grief that comes before the ending, during illness, dementia, or long decline. You lose someone slowly, in pieces.

Example:
A daughter watches her father fade through Alzheimer's and mourns the man he once was, long before his final breath.

The Six Stages: A Language for Understanding Grief

Elisabeth Kübler-Ross forever changed the landscape of grief education. Her work didn't just introduce concepts; it gave the world a way to name what had always been wordless, chaotic, and intensely private.

Her model centered on five stages of grief, based on her extensive work with patients who were facing the end of their lives. These stages were never intended to be linear or prescriptive. Rather, they were an acknowledgment of the emotional honesty that so many people felt but had no language for.

Years later, David Kessler, who worked closely with Kübler-Ross until her death, continued her legacy. Through thousands of hours with grieving individuals and families, he expanded her framework by introducing a sixth stage: Finding Meaning.

This was not a replacement for her work; it was a continuation of it. A way to honor what grief becomes over time.

Together, the six stages offer a compassionate language for understanding grief: not as something to fix or rush through, but as something to honor.

Here they are with the depth they deserve:

1. Denial "This can't be happening."

Kübler-Ross taught us that denial is not a refusal to face reality.
It is the psyche's first, instinctive shield — a temporary buffer that protects the heart from breaking all at once. Denial allows us to absorb the truth only in pieces as we are able.
When Will died, denial gave me breath when everything else inside me collapsed.

2. Anger "Why? Why now? Why us?"

In Kübler-Ross's original model, anger was never a sign of failure — it was a sign of connection.
Anger is the fire that rises when love has nowhere to land.
It is the soul's insistence that the loss was real, that the bond mattered, that the world has been altered.

Anger says: *This mattered.*

3. Bargaining "If only ... maybe if I ..."

Kübler-Ross described bargaining as the mind's attempt to negotiate with reality.
It is not irrational — it is deeply human.
When life feels unbearable, the mind reaches for any thread of control:
a rewrite, a bargain, a wish, a plea.
Bargaining is longing disguised as logic.

4. Depression "I can't do this."

Traditional culture often pathologizes depression, but Kübler-Ross understood it differently.
In grief, depression is a valid and necessary emotional descent, the body and soul acknowledging the full weight of the loss.
It is honesty, not illness.
A slowing down that says, *This is heavy, and I need rest.*
It is often in this quiet depth that the seeds of meaning begin to take root.

5. Acceptance "This is my reality."

Acceptance is the final stage in Kübler-Ross's original model.
It is not an agreement.
It is not approved.
It is not being "okay" with what happened.
Acceptance is simply the softening into truth: the moment you stop fighting reality and begin learning how to live with it.
It is not the end of grief, but the beginning of living alongside it.

6. Finding Meaning "The love that stays."

This sixth stage was later introduced by David Kessler, grounded in decades of his own clinical and personal experience.
Meaning doesn't diminish the pain: it gives the pain direction. It honors love by allowing it to shape how we move forward. Meaning is where grief is transformed, not erased.

For me, finding meaning meant choosing to carry Will's love into my work, and into my everyday life, through service, truth-telling, and walking with others as they rise from their own valleys.

Meaning is not a solution. Meaning is purpose emerging from the broken pieces. It is where grief becomes sacred.

A Client Story: Sandra's Grief Through Divorce

Sandra came to me after the end of her twenty-two-year marriage. On the outside, the divorce looked almost civil: two adults dividing a life, signing documents, making plans, and trying to be "mature" about it. But inside? She was wrecked. Completely undone.

In our first session, she looked down at her hands, shoulders curled inward as if she were trying to make herself smaller. "I feel stupid grieving this," she said quietly, almost apologizing for the words as they came out.

She truly believed grief was reserved for funerals and cemeteries.
She believed that because her ex-husband was still breathing, her sorrow didn't qualify.
She thought her heartache was somehow less legitimate.

But grief doesn't care about technicalities.
Grief doesn't rank suffering.
Grief responds to attachment, to love, to the fabric of your life being torn.

And Sandra had lost a lot.

She lost her identity as a wife.
She lost the comfort of those familiar morning routines.
She lost the future she had built in her mind for over two decades.
She lost the tenderness of being known by someone who had witnessed her entire adult life.
She lost companionship, the daily "I'm home," the shared grocery lists, the boring little rituals that end up meaning everything.

She wasn't just grieving a person.
She was grieving a *world.*

As we worked together, I watched her move through the stages of grief in the only way any of us do: messily, beautifully, one breath at a time.

There were moments of denial: "Maybe he'll come back once things settle."
There were fiery waves of anger: "Why do I have to rebuild from scratch while he gets to reinvent himself?"
There were nights of bargaining: "If I had just been more patient … maybe …"
There were heavy days of depression when she said, "I don't even know who I am without this relationship."

And then, eventually, there was acceptance—not with a smile, not with relief, but with honesty: "It's over. And I have to figure out who I am now."

But my favorite moment came months later, in a session where she sat a little taller, let out a sigh, and with a tinge of a smile, she said:

"I survived. And I finally see myself. And I know I want more, I deserve more than this."

Not triumphant.
Not tied up with a pretty bow.
Just the truth. And hope. And grace.

Her grief wasn't smaller because time had passed, and as she said, "It's not like anyone died or anything." Her grief was sacred because it was *hers*.
It deserved space. It deserved tenderness. It deserved honoring.

And she did the brave work of learning how to honor it: to let grace in.

The Alchemy of Loss

Grief is one of the few forces powerful enough to break you open and remake you simultaneously. It dismantles your identity, your assumptions, your sense of safety. And then, slowly and gently, it invites you to rebuild from the inside out.

Not back to who you were.
But forward into who you're becoming.

Grief is not a detour from life; it is an invitation into a deeper one.

You discover:

- Love didn't vanish
- Grace didn't disappear
- God didn't leave.
- You are still here
- And something in you refuses to surrender

This is where grace works its quiet alchemy, in the breaking, in the bewilderment, in the truth that you were never meant to carry this alone.

Grief cracks the heart open.
Grace flows through the cracks.

Reflection Questions

1. Which type of grief is present for you right now: death, identity, relationship, invisible grief, or the loss of a dream? What is one way you can honor it without minimizing or apologizing for it?

2. Where in your grief journey have you been unexpectedly "sent back to the beginning," and how can you offer yourself radical compassion for the nonlinear path you're walking?

3. If finding meaning is the sixth stage, what is one small choice, practice, or act of courage that could help your pain move toward purpose—even if only by one inch today?

How We Grieve: No Wrong Way

There's no universal language for grief.
Some people cry; others clean. Some talk; others go silent. Some run; others rest.

Over the years, I've seen five "grief languages":

- **The Doer** stays in motion: organizing, planning, solving.
- **The Feeler** lets the emotions wash through tears, journaling, and connection.
- **The Thinker** studies the pain, reading, researching, seeking to understand.
- **The Seeker** searches for spiritual meaning.
- **The Withdrawer** goes inward to process in solitude.

None of these is wrong. They're simply the body and soul doing what they must to survive what feels unsurvivable. The invitation is to notice how *you* grieve, and to let it be enough.

Finding Meaning: The Stage That Saves Us

For me, meaning didn't arrive as a revelation; it came as a series of fragile choices: to keep breathing, to keep living, to keep showing up, even though it felt totally wrong at a soul level to do so. I began to see that the love I shared with Will hadn't disappeared; it had changed form.
Even though part of me died with him, another part was reborn, not through triumph, but through tears and trembling surrender.

Finding meaning became my lifeline, the thread that tethered me to love, to God, to the belief that I could turn my pain into purpose.
Meaning didn't erase the ache. It simply gave the pain somewhere sacred to go.

Chapter 7

The Ways We Avoid Grief (And Why None of Them Mean We're Broken)

Grief has a way of breaking through everything we pretend to be.

One moment, we're moving through life like a champ, managing responsibilities, making plans, keeping it together, and then something cracks open. A loss, a diagnosis, a heartbreak, a betrayal, a death, a dream collapsing. Suddenly, our insides feel rearranged, and the world looks different in a way we can't un-see.

Most people think grief is just sadness, when in fact, grief is way more complicated than that.
Grief is a full-body experience. It hits your heart, your sleep, your work, your relationships, your faith, your future, and your sense of self. It messes with your appetite, your energy, and your memory. It presses on places you didn't know were tender. So, of course, we may try to outrun it or deny its entry, not because we're weak or uncaring, but because our hearts are wired to protect us from too much pain at once.

This chapter is not about shaming us. It's about understanding who we are, who we were. Because when we recognize the ways we avoid grief, we can stop beating ourselves up and slowly start meeting ourselves with compassion. When we know more, when we feel safe enough to go there, the grip of grief, whether conscious or not, can slowly begin to loosen.

How We Cope When the Pain Feels Too Big

The patterns listed below, the ones I see in my clients, in my community, and in myself, are not failures. They are survival strategies. And like any survival tool, they work for us … until they don't. As you read through the list, remember that we all cope in different ways. How you've handled your loss is personal, and it deserves tenderness, not shame or guilt.

1. Busyness: The socially acceptable numbing device

Let's start with the coping mechanism that gets applause: staying busy. Our culture loves a productive person. We reward the ones who push through, show up, and never miss a beat. I've done this one. Many times. Sometimes it wasn't even intentional—my nervous system simply didn't want to be still. When we're constantly moving, we never have to sit long enough to feel the earthquake under our feet. Busyness becomes armor. It looks strong and admirable, but often it's just fear dressed up in a power suit.

2. Distraction & Numbing

We're naturals at this, maybe too good. 😉 Scrolling, eating, not eating, drinking, weed, shopping, cleaning, staying up late, signing up for five new commitments you don't even want. Numbing isn't always destructive; sometimes it's simply a way to turn the emotional volume down. A temporary anesthetic. But the ache waits patiently for its turn.

3. Becoming the Helper Instead of the Hurt One

When life hurts, many of us slip into roles like the fixer, the coach, the leader, the caretaker. We say, "I've got you," instead of "I'm not okay." Helping others can be holy work, but it can also become a hiding place. When we're the strong ones, we don't have to feel our own collapse.

4. Shutting Down

Some people do the opposite. They withdraw. They go quiet. They lose energy, interest, or desire. They disappear inside themselves. This is not laziness, and it's not always depression. Often, it's the body saying: *We need to conserve energy because something enormous is happening inside.* There is wisdom in a shutdown. It's the nervous system choosing stillness over overload.

5. Intellectualizing or Spiritualizing

This one is sneaky—especially for thinkers, the faith-filled, the self-aware, and those who have read all the books. We analyze instead of feeling. We hunt for lessons instead of sitting with the wound. We jump to meaning too fast. And in spiritual spaces, we wrap our suffering in holy words: "God is working," "There must be a reason," "There's a plan here." Beautiful truths, yes. But when used too early, they become a bypass, not a balm. God is not afraid of your grief. You don't have to tidy it up before bringing it to Him.

6. Anger as a Bodyguard

Anger is clean, energizing, and protective. Grief is slow, vulnerable, and heavy. So the brain often chooses anger—it feels safer. Anger says, "Don't come closer. Don't ask questions. Don't touch the tenderness underneath." If you're snapping, irritated, resentful, or wanting to throw something, congratulations: you're grieving. Anger isn't wrong; it's just not the whole story. Beneath every anger is a loss that mattered.

7. Control: The Illusion that Keeps Us Functioning

Loss takes away control, so we try to reclaim it wherever we can. We micromanage meals, routines, calendars, conversations, people's emotions, the way the dishwasher is loaded—anything we can grip with our hands. It's the brain saying, "If I can't change what broke me, let me manage something." But control isn't safety. It only feels like it for a moment.

8. Forced Positivity

This is the bright-side strategy. We smile. We say we're fine. We insist on gratitude while our heart bleeds. We avoid anything that might "bring the mood down." Forced positivity isn't hope. It's self-protection. True hope has room for honesty.

9. Comparison

Comparison is a quiet self-abandonment. We tell ourselves, "Others have it worse," "I shouldn't feel this way," "People survive harder things." Comparison shrinks the truth of your pain. Grief does not require justification.

10. Perfectionism

We try to hold everything together, to be composed, capable, and strong. Perfectionism is control dressed up as virtue. It whispers, "If I do everything perfectly, maybe nothing else will fall apart." But perfection has never saved a soul. Grace has.

11. Minimizing

We downplay the loss. We rationalize it. We talk ourselves out of our own heartbreak. But the body always knows the truth, even when the mind is trying to explain it away.

12. Isolation or Over-Socializing

Isolation says, "If I stay alone, no one will see how much I'm hurting."
Over-socializing says, "If I stay constantly surrounded, I'll never have to be alone with myself."
Both responses are rooted in fear. Both are understandable. Neither is failure.

13. Losing Yourself in Someone Else

This can look like diving into a new relationship, attaching quickly, people-pleasing, over-connecting, or becoming dependent on someone else's presence. It's a way to avoid the void—a way to fill the space left behind. But no one else's voice can take the place of your own.

14. Over-Strength

This one gets so many of us, especially those who've built lives on grit and resilience. The strength that carried you through earlier battles becomes armor in grief. And that armor gets unbearably heavy when worn too long. True strength isn't the refusal to feel. It's the willingness to.

Ugh, so ... what do we do with all this?

I know, painful, right? Even writing this chapter was hard. That rush of recognition, that moment of, *"Wow... that's still me."*

So what do we do with that?
We start by telling ourselves he truth gently and without judgment. The simple truth we've been avoiding: "I'm hurting, and this is how I have handled my hurt."

And you know what? That's okay. We did our best with what we had. This kind of understanding lets light reach the places we weren't ready to face before. So go gently here, my friend.

Part one is simply recognizing our avoidance strategies. Most of us use more than one. Sometimes we use several at once. That's just being human. And when we can name the ways we're trying to protect ourselves, whether through busyness, caretaking, numbing, control, over-strength, or anything else, we create the first crack to let the light of grace in.

The next step is slowing down enough to feel what's underneath. Not all at once. Not without support. But slowly, gently, intentionally. Healing grief begins when we allow ourselves to experience it in the presence of safety, with a therapist, a coach, a grief group, trusted friends, or a community that can hold what we carry.

Because grief was never meant to be carried alone.
Healing happens when we are willing to witness our grief, and just as importantly, when we allow others to witness it with us.

You don't have to fix yourself.
You don't have to rush.
You don't have to be brave every minute.

You're not doing grief wrong.
You're human.
And letting yourself be seen in your grief is the first real opening toward healing and letting the love in.

Reflection Questions

1. Which of these coping strategies do you recognize in yourself right now?

2. Where do you notice yourself avoiding the deeper ache?

3. What might it feel like to soften, even 1%, into that grief instead of running from it?

4. Who are the safest people for you to share the unedited version of your pain with?

5. What is grief trying to reveal to you about what mattered?

Chapter 8

The 7-Step Grief Integration Process

This is not a formula, and it's not a fix. It's a pathway: a way to move with grief rather than fight it, fear it, or run from it. Think of these steps as invitations to your healing process, not as requirements

1. Name the Loss Honestly (Truth Before Transformation)

Most people skip this part. They jump to meaning, strength, or caretaking. But healing begins by naming what changed.

Ask yourself:

- What exactly did I lose?
- What part of me is grieving?
- What dream, relationship, identity, or expectation was broken?

Grief isn't only about death; it's about anything that will never be the same again.
Naming it anchors the process, so we open ourselves up to let grace in.

2. Notice Your Grief Protectors Without Shame

We all have patterns that try to shield us from overwhelm.

These patterns aren't signs that something is wrong with us; they're signs that something inside us is hurting. They form because the heart is trying to survive what the mind can't yet fully face.

These include:

- Busyness
- Numbing
- Control
- Caretaking
- Perfectionism
- Anger
- Isolation
- Over-spiritualizing
- Over-strength

These are not failures. They are attempts to keep us safe.

Say to yourself:
"This is how my system protects me when the pain feels too big."

Awareness softens resistance.
Resistance softens suffering.

3. Give Your Body a Moment to Speak (Even 90 Seconds)

Neuroscientist Dr. Jill Bolte Taylor discovered that the lifespan of an emotion, the pure physiological wave, is only about 90 seconds. That's all it takes for the chemicals to surge, rise, peak, and settle in the body. After those 90 seconds, the physical emotion has completed its cycle.

So why do our feelings sometimes last all day, or keep coming back again and again? Because we unintentionally re-trigger the emotional wave with our thoughts: the memories, fears, worries, and stories we attach to the sensation. The emotion ends, but the loop continues. This isn't a flaw. It's simply how the human brain works when it's trying to protect us.

The wisdom here is simple and incredibly freeing: if you can give your body even 90 seconds of presence, the wave can move through you. Grief shifts. The nervous system resets. You don't have to control the feeling or suppress it. You only have to allow one wave to complete, no matter how powerful it may feel .. Your body knows how to carry you through it, and it will, if you let it.

Try:

- Sitting in silence
- Placing a hand on your heart
- Letting one tear fall
- Breathing through the tightness
- Saying a single honest sentence

It takes courage to feel your feelings. Let the wave crest and fall. You will be ok.

4. Let Others In (Strength Was Never Meant to Be Done Alone)

Grief isolates. Healing doesn't.

Grief pulls us inward and makes us believe we have to carry it alone. But healing begins the moment we let someone step into the darkness with us. Not to rescue us, but to be a witness to our experience. Choose one safe person:

- A friend
- A therapist
- A coach
- A pastor
- A grief group
- Someone who simply listens

Say: “I’m not okay, and I don’t want to hold this alone.”

Connection regulates the nervous system.
Grief shared allows grace to perform it’s magic.

5. Create Rituals That Honor What Was Lost

Ritual gives pain somewhere to go. It takes what the heart has been holding, quietly, heavily, and makes it real. Something you can name. Something you can honor. Without it, grief spills everywhere. Ritual contains it. You might:

- Write a letter
- Visit a meaningful place
- Light a candle
- Say their name
- Tell the story

- Keep a significant object
- Create art, prayer, or movement dedicated to them

Ritual anchors meaning without forcing healing. It's your heart saying: "This mattered. And it still does."

6. Allow the Grief to Change You (The Identity Shift)

Every loss creates a before and an after.

It alters your inner landscape in ways you can't fully see at first. Over time, you begin to understand that grief didn't just break you: it reshaped you.

Ask:

- Who am I now?
- What part of me is being reshaped?
- What truth can I no longer ignore?
- What new values or boundaries are emerging?

Grief isn't only about letting go, it's about becoming. You don't return to who you were.
You grow into who you are now.

7. Integrate Grace (The Ongoing Practice of Living Forward)

Grief doesn't disappear, but it does integrate.
It becomes something you walk with instead of something you're crushed under. It rises and falls, but it no longer takes you out. It becomes a quiet companion that reminds you of how deeply you loved.

Grace shows up when you:

- Breathe easier
- Remember without collapsing
- Take one small step into the future
- Forgive yourself
- Loosen the armor
- Let joy coexist with sorrow

Grace shows up when grief is allowed to move instead of being buried. When pain has somewhere to go instead of getting locked inside you.

This is where something important becomes clear:
The love didn't die.
The relationship didn't disappear, it changed form.
And you're still here, with a life that isn't finished yet.

Chapter 9

The Griefs We Don't Talk About

Not all grief begins with a funeral or ends with closure.
Some grief is loud and visible; some hides under years of responsibility and quiet endurance.

Some grief arrives slowly, like fog that never lifts. Other times, it hits like an explosion, like what I referenced in an earlier chapter, the Grief Bomb. It levels everything you thought was safe.

We often imagine grief as a single event, something we "go through" and then recover from, but grief is not a straight line. It's a landscape. It loops, it lingers, it doubles back. It waits until life slows down enough for it to finally be felt.

And some griefs, the ones we don't name or believe we're not entitled to feel, are the ones that shape us most.

Delayed Grief

Delayed grief is what happens when we can't afford to fall apart when loss first arrives.
You keep going, hold everyone else together, stay in motion. Your heart whispers, *not now,* and your body listens.

But grief waits. It surfaces months or even years later, in tears you can't explain, in irritability, in a sudden sadness that feels out of place. That's delayed grief: pain postponed until you have the strength to face it.

It's not weakness, it's how the human spirit protects itself. Healing begins the moment you stop apologizing for still feeling what others think you should be "over."

Compounded Grief

Compounded grief happens when losses stack up before you've had a chance to recover from the first.
A loved one dies. A relationship ends. You lose your health, your job, your sense of identity, all before the first wound has even closed.

Eventually, it all blends. You stop knowing what you're grieving and just feel heavy all the time. It's disorienting. But it's also normal. Life doesn't always give us space to heal one loss before the next arrives.

What helps is naming the weight honestly: *This is too much.* That truth, unfiltered, unedited, is the beginning of compassion. Because you can't care for yourself in grief until you stop pretending you're fine.

Traumatic Grief

Some losses don't just break your heart; they break your sense of safety. When loss comes through violence, suicide, or sudden tragedy, it doesn't only take the person you love; it can take your ability to trust the world.

Traumatic grief is grief mixed with shock.
It's the sleeplessness, the racing thoughts, the flashbacks, the sense that life stopped and never restarted. You're not just mourning who you lost, you're mourning the version of you that believed life made sense.

Healing this kind of grief takes time, patience, and often trauma-informed support. It's not about "getting over it." It's about learning how to carry what happened without letting it carry you.
Even small acts of safety, grounding in your breath, connecting with a trusted person, talking openly without fear of judgment, begin to loosen trauma's grip.

You can't fix what happened, but you can learn to live *through* it.
And that, in itself, is sacred work.

The Hidden Griefs

Not every loss comes with condolences or casseroles.
There's the grief of identity: who you used to be before life changed.
The grief of growing older in a culture that pretends aging is optional.
The grief of faith lost, friendship faded, dreams that never found form.

These quiet losses are easy to overlook, even by us. But when ignored, they grow heavier. The truth is, grief ignored doesn't disappear; it waits for acknowledgment.
Naming it is what frees it.

Write it down. Speak it aloud. Share it with someone who won't try to fix you. Let your grief be witnessed. Because healing doesn't happen in isolation: it happens in connection.

When we allow someone to hold space for our pain, the burden shifts, even if only slightly. That's how the heart begins to make room again for life.

Choosing to Live

After a deep loss, there's a difference between being alive and *living*.
In the beginning, you survive, you breathe, you function, you do what has to be done.
But there comes a time when you realize survival alone isn't enough.

Choosing to live isn't some dramatic comeback story. It's persistent. It's unglamorous. It's making breakfast when you don't care if you eat. It's answering a text you'd rather avoid. It's stepping outside because staying inside feels like it might close in on you. It's choosing connection even when pulling away feels easier.

Sometimes the way back to life isn't about fixing yourself at all. It's about doing something kind while you're still cracked open. Helping someone else. Volunteering. Listening to another person's story without trying to solve it. Those things become bridges. Not because they erase your grief, but because they remind you that you're still here, and that you still have something to offer.

Giving doesn't cancel grief. It gives it somewhere to go.

There's no tidy middle ground when it comes to living. You engage, or you drift. And engaging doesn't mean being cheerful or optimistic or healed. It means taking one small action that keeps you tethered to life, even when life feels messy.

The minute you decide to step back in, awkwardly, imperfectly, on your own terms, something starts to shift. Not because you stop missing what you lost, but because you remember this: love didn't end. It still exists on this side of loss.

And grace, quiet, mysterious, unannounced, meets you there.

Reflection Questions

1. What part of your grief still needs to be witnessed, by yourself or by someone you trust?

2. Where might an act of kindness, even small, begin to reconnect you with the living world?

3. What does choosing to live look like for you today?

Chapter 10

The Body Keeps the Score

Grief doesn't just break the heart; it moves through the body and often settles there.
It nestles into places we don't always recognize or understand. It shows up in the catch of the breath, the tightness in the chest, the heaviness that hits without warning. It hides inside the joints, the muscles, the nervous system.

Our bodies remember everything: the love, the loss, the longing, and the shock of being asked to keep living after the world has shifted under our feet.

After the loss of my brother, and years later, the loss of my son, the gym became my sanctuary. Not everyone wants to lift heavy, and not everyone needs to. But for me, pushing weight was the thing that kept me sane. It gave me a place to put the ache, a place to breathe, and a place where my body could express what my heart couldn't yet speak. It wasn't elegant, mindful, or gentle. It was survival: a rhythm and structure that helped me stay tethered to myself when everything else felt like it was ripped away from me.

But here's what grief taught me and what I now teach the people I walk with: grief is not only emotional. It's physical. And the body often knows we're grieving long before we have the words for it. The body is grief's scorekeeper.

Which brings us to you: your body, your signals, your wisdom.

How Grief Shows Up in the Body

Grief speaks through the body long before you are aware of it. You may notice:

- **Tightness or clenching**
Your body is bracing to protect your heart. Shoulders rising. Jaw gripping. Chest guarded.

- **Restlessness or agitation**
Pacing, fidgeting, trouble sitting still, that buzzing-under-the-skin feeling. This is your nervous system searching for release.

- **Sudden fatigue or emotional crashes**
Energy dropping out of nowhere. Exhaustion you can't explain. The body says, "Something inside needs attention."

- **Stomach knots, nausea, or digestive shifts**
The gut holds grief- appetite changes, tension, discomfort, bloating, an "off" feeling with no clear cause.

- **Back pain, shoulder pain, or neck tension**
We blame the pillow, the workout, or a long day, but these areas often store sorrow, responsibility, and unexpressed emotion.

- **Headaches or pressure behind the eyes**
Not always screens or dehydration, sometimes grief trying to surface.

- **Heaviness in the limbs or a weight in the chest**
The physical sensation of emotional weight.

- **Moments of unexpected strength or clarity**
The body remembers resilience.
These flashes aren't signs you're "over it", they're part of how your body supports you.

Each sensation is communication. Your body isn't failing you; it's pointing you toward what needs: tenderness, presence, or release.

When the Body Tells the Truth: Two Stories

Grief doesn't show up the same way for everyone. Some people carry it in their inability to take a deep breath; others carry it in their backs, joints, stomachs, or shoulders. Two clients I worked with showed me this in powerful ways.

Maria came to me after losing her mother. She didn't say she was grieving; she said she "didn't feel like herself." Her shoulders were always lifted, her breath shallow, her energy low. She thought it was stress, hormones, or being overextended. But through deeper questioning and gentle somatic breath work, as I invited her to place a hand on her heart and breathe, she froze. Tears filled her eyes as she whispered,
"Why does this feel like I'm going to break?"

I told her softly, "Because your body has been holding what your heart hasn't felt safe enough to say." Her entire posture softened, as if her body finally had permission to exhale. Tears came to her eyes. She finally felt safe enough to express what her body was holding. That moment didn't "fix" her grief, it simply opened the door for it to be expressed.

Jim's grief showed up differently. In our Zoom sessions, he kept talking about how his back "kept going out." Every week he'd say, "I must've slept weird," or "I must've tweaked something." But one afternoon, during our weekly call, he paused, looked away from the screen, then came back with tears in his eyes and said quietly: "I don't understand why everything hurts."

I told him gently, "Because you're carrying something, and your heart hasn't felt safe enough to feel it yet." And then I saw it: the shift, not an unraveling, but recognition. Jim wasn't falling apart. He was grieving. He was finally coming home to himself.

Both of these clients taught me, and now model for you, that grief rarely screams in ways we can know or understand. It often waits in our body in disguise as tension, fatigue, pain, pressure, numbness, or overwhelm. And when we finally slow down enough to listen, the body becomes the place where grief steps forward and gently says, *"I've been here the whole time. I am really glad you are here."*

Because the body is more than a collection of muscles and nerves: it is the holy vessel we were given to experience life. The joy, the heartbreak, the longing, the love, the loss- all of it flows through this one sacred place we inhabit. And when we honor the body through our struggles, we honor the life we've lived, the love we've carried, and the grief that has shaped us. The body was never the problem. It has always been the portal back to ourselves.

Somatic Practices That Bring You Back Into Your Body

We all heal differently. There's no single right way. What matters is staying in your body, not abandoning it.

Here are pathways back to yourself:

- **Yoga**- noticing where grief sits through stretches, whether in a class or alone.
- **Somatic dance or intuitive movement**- letting the body say what the mouth cannot.
- **Hiking or slow walking**- letting steady steps and nature calm the nervous system.
- **Strength training**- giving emotional pressure a physical outlet to release.
- **Massage or bodywork**- releasing stored tension and grief pockets through movement of the body tissue.

- **Breathwork**- teaching your lungs to expand again, to breathe fully- to release and let go.
- **Reiki or energy work**- for gentle relief when you feel fragile.
- **Stretching**- softening the armor grief builds and allowing free movement to connect you back to your body. You can do this in bed, in a chair, at the kitchen counter. Movement is medicine.
- **Sauna, cold plunges, warm baths**- changing your state, re-regulating the nervous system, relaxation, awakening.
- **Praying, meditating-** being fully present in the moment with your breath is often the most healing modality of them all.

None of these practices "fix" grief. But they do give grief a place to flow, instead of staying trapped inside you. What I know for sure: movement is medicine. We cannot heal what we do not allow to release through our body.

Leaning Into the Light

Healing isn't about forcing pain away. It's about creating enough safety inside your body for light to return, even in small moments. When you walk, lift, stretch, breathe, dance, or simply pause with intention, you remind your body:

You can hold sorrow and still be alive.
You can grieve and still move.
You can hurt and still heal.

Movement becomes a bridge:
from numbness to feeling,
from tension to release,
from isolation to connection,
from darkness to a faint glimmer of light

From Grief to Grace.

Your body knows things your mind isn't ready to say. It tells you when to rest, when to cry, when to move, and when to rise. And when you listen, it becomes your most faithful guide back to yourself.

Reflection Questions

1. Where and how do you feel grief in your body right now: tight, heavy, buzzing, restless, tired?

2. Which movements or somatic practices help you feel more connected? What modality mentioned above are you willing to explore?

3. Are you willing to be curious that a pain or tension you are experiencing may be emotional rather than physical?

4. Where could you allow in even a small dose of light: sunlight, warmth, music, touch, fresh air, connection?

5. What might your body be trying to tell you that your mind hasn't acknowledged yet?

Chapter 11

The Process of Becoming

The Psychology of Grief and the Science of Change

Grief and change follow the same basic rules.

Both disrupt who we think we are.
Both shake the stories we've been telling ourselves.
Both force us to adapt, whether we're ready or not.

From a psychological standpoint, grief isn't just about sadness or loss. It hits the whole system. Your nervous system. Your sense of safety. Your motivation. Your memory. Your identity. It changes how you experience the world and how you experience yourself. In that way, grief isn't separate from change; it's one of the most powerful forces for it.

The science of change tells us something most of us don't love to hear: people rarely change because they feel inspired. They change because something stops working. A role. A strategy. A way of coping. Growth usually doesn't start with clarity—it starts when the old way falls apart.

That's why grief is so destabilizing.

It removes the structures that once helped us function. The roles we leaned on. The beliefs that made life feel predictable. The internal rules that told us who we were and how things were supposed to work. When those fall apart, we're left exposed, without the usual tools we use to manage uncertainty.

And humans respond to that exposure in pretty predictable ways. Some of us tighten control. Some stay busy. Some overperform. Some shut down. Some intellectualize. Some spiritualize. None of this means something is wrong with you. These are survival strategies. They're the nervous system doing its best to keep us upright.

No one is immune to this.

What we often call personality is really just adaptation under pressure.

Grief, however, has a way of overwhelming even our best strategies. Insight doesn't protect you from it. Success doesn't insulate you. Intelligence doesn't outmaneuver it. At some point, managing stops working, and a deeper kind of change begins—not because you chose it, but because you have to live forward somehow.

This is the process of becoming.

Not going back to who you were.
Not fixing what broke.
But slowly, honestly, being shaped into someone new.

Healing isn't mechanical.
It isn't linear.
And it isn't something you complete.

It's human.
It's relational.
It's alive.

Long before grief entered my life in the way it eventually would, I was already paying close attention to how people work. I've always been fascinated by human behavior, how we respond when things get hard, what we do to cope, and what shows up when we're not trying to hold it all together. Even my theater training wasn't really about performing for me; it was about observing. Being fully present. Learning how to notice what's happening underneath the words.

That curiosity has been there forever. Ever since I could read, I found myself wandering straight to the psychology and spirituality sections of any library I walked into. And I walked into a lot of libraries. I still love them. There's something comforting about being surrounded by all the ways humans have tried to understand ourselves, how we suffer, how we grow, how we make meaning when life doesn't follow the plan.

I've always loved being around kids for the same reason. They're honest. Direct. What you see is what you get. Before we learn how to manage impressions or smooth things over, kids show you exactly what's there, curiosity, fear, joy, sadness, all of it, right on the surface.

As adults, we lose some of that openness. Not because anything is wrong with us, but because life teaches us how to cope. How to stay functional. How to keep going. Those skills matter. They help us survive. But grief has a way of cutting straight through them.

When grief shows up, observation alone doesn't carry you through. Insight doesn't protect you. Presence doesn't stop the pain. Even knowing a lot about grief doesn't keep you from being changed by it. At some point, you're no longer studying the process, you're inside it.

And that's when becoming stops being theoretical and starts being real.

The Intersection of Psychology and the Soul

I've been in the world of coaching and behavioral change long enough to know this: growth is both an art and a science.

Psychology gives us language for what our hearts already know: that change is rarely clean or follows a straight line. It's slow. Awkward. Usually happening right in the middle of a mess, not after everything has been all tidied up.

In behavioral theory, we talk about stages: *awareness, preparation, action, and integration.*
Which sounds very professional. I tend to think of them more like this: *Oh no. Fine, I'll try. This is terrible. Okay … maybe I'm not dying after all.* 😉

Grief, in its own way, follows a similar pattern.

First there's *denial*: that stunned sense of *this can't be real.* Then *resistance*: the pushback against what we can't control, can't fix, can't undo. Eventually, there's a kind of vague, almost surreal phase of *acceptance*, where we start figuring out how to live inside a world that doesn't look or feel the way it used to.

Some days you feel like you're making progress. Other days you're crying at a red light or standing in the grocery store because a random song comes on and hits you right where it hurts. That's not failure. That's not regression. That's what transformation actually looks like.

Behavioral science calls this *integration.* Grief calls it *acceptance.* But they're really pointing to the same thing: learning how to live inside what's true now. Not returning to who we were before, but becoming who we're meant to be next. Even if we are dragging our heels through the process.

The Myth of Closure

Which brings me to one of the biggest myths we're sold.

The myth of closure.

What does that even mean, anyway? As if grief comes with a completion date. As if one day you wake up, check a box, and think, *Great, I'm done missing them now.*

I once had a client say, half-joking and half-exhausted, "I just want closure so I can stop feeling sad." And I remember gently asking her, "What would that look like?" She paused and said, "I guess … not caring anymore?" We both sat in silence for a moment. And she added, "But I will always care: My biggest fear is that I will forget …"

What she wanted wasn't necessarily closure. It was some form of relief. It was the ability to live again without feeling like grief was waiting like a steamroller. Putting truth to our fears alleviates the pain in some way, because speaking into our longing helps us far more than what people realize. I know that was certainly true for me.

Yet, society tells us that if we stay positive, work hard enough, or follow the right steps, we'll eventually arrive at this neat, finished place called *closure*. It sounds comforting. Manageable. Like something you can file away and move past.

But grief doesn't close. It deepens. It changes shape.

And change doesn't end. It keeps unfolding.

What actually happens, if we're honest, is something quieter and more human. Acceptance begins to form, but it's mixed with longing. Melancholy softens, but it doesn't disappear. And alongside it, almost surprisingly, a small seed of hope starts to grow. Not the loud, motivational kind. The steady kind. The kind that says, *I can carry this and still keep living.*

This is where the soul does its quiet work. It integrates what was lost without erasing it. It learns how to hold grief and life at the same time. It perseveres, not by forcing positivity, but by staying present.

The goal isn't to fix what's broken. It's to let what's been broken teach us how to live differently. That's what real growth is: a continual conversation between pain and possibility.

And the work, the real, gritty, human work, isn't about rushing through the mess. It's about staying with it just long enough to hear what it's trying to show you.

The Day the Armor Cracked

Not long ago, I was speaking at a conference, one of those spiffy business events where everyone's dressed sharp and looks like they have it all together.

I was on a panel with three other speakers, and something about one of the women beside me caught my attention. She had that same polished exterior we all wear in those settings, but underneath, I could feel something- a depth, a weight, a knowing.

After the panel, when the microphones were off and the heels were starting to hurt, she turned to me and said softly, "I need to tell you something."

Her sister had died suddenly in a car accident. When you talked about the loss of your son, I knew you knew my loss, and I just wanted to share my story with you.

In that instant, the whole vibe shifted. The air got quieter. We cried. We hugged. We ruined our makeup. And standing there, side by side, we were talking as humans who had been broken open by loss.

Grief does that. It opens us, allows us the sacred position to be a witness to the grief of another.

It strips away the small talk and gets right to the truth of things. You'll notice that once you've lived through real loss, people start telling you things: deep, personal things, in the grocery line, on airplanes, in between sessions at conferences. They sense it. They can feel that you're someone who can hold their story without flinching.

And maybe that's one of the quiet gifts of grief, it makes us more available, more compassionate, more real to the struggle of others.

Becoming Whole Again

Grace and support help, of course. So do the tools we can use to cope: journaling, prayer, therapy, movement, community, faith. But these strategies aren't solutions; they're companions in our healing.

What changes us isn't the tools themselves, but our willingness to use them honestly: to be willing to stop pretending we're fine, to let others in, and to allow our new life to remake us slowly from the inside out.

Real healing, like real change, isn't about becoming who we were before the loss. It's about becoming who we are now- wiser, softer, maybe even weirder, more human because we dare to stay with what is real. To stay is not easy. But it is so worth it.

And through the staying, we learn that it's okay to laugh in the middle of the tears. That humor is holy, too. And that maybe, just maybe, with grace as our guide, we can begin the process of putting ourselves back together, less neat and tidy, more open, more real.

Reflection Questions

1. Where in your life are you still trying to "fix" something that might instead be asking to be felt or accepted?

2. What practices or supports help you stay present when you want to rush ahead or shut down?

3. How might grace be inviting you, not to control the process, but to trust the unfolding of who you're becoming?

Chapter 12

Emotional Entanglements

How Loss Rewrites Our Attachments

Grief changes the landscape of our relationships, whether we want it to or not. The world tilts. The people in it look different, not because they changed, but because we did. Loss recalibrates your internal compass. It clarifies what you need, strips away what you can no longer fake, and forces a level of honesty you didn't ask for but can't unsee once it arrives.

Some people pull away. Others draw closer. A few surprise you with just a steady, calm presence. And some reveal their limits: their discomfort, their avoidance, their inability to stay. Grief doesn't just show you who people are; it shows you what they're capable of.

As we relearn who we are after loss, we start asking for things we never would have voiced before: space, support, clarity, truth. We say what we need out loud because silence no longer protects us. It only isolates us.

And with that clarity often comes a wave of something that can feel unfamiliar: righteousness, even indignation. Not arrogance. Truth. A deep internal knowing that says, *I can't pretend anymore. I won't shrink anymore. I can't carry your expectations while I'm rebuilding myself.*

These aren't overreactions.
They're boundaries forged in heartbreak.

But not everyone's grief rises like that.

For many, the shift turns inward. They don't feel righteous; they feel tender. Quiet. Wounded. They question themselves, wondering if they're being too sensitive or too changed. They might withdraw, speak less, or feel everything more deeply under the surface. This internal version of grief is just as valid, just as real, and just as transformative. Some roar. Some barely make a peep.

Both are grief speaking.

And what I learned through my own losses is that this part often adds an unexpected layer to the grief itself. It's confusing. We think, *"How could they not know? How could they not see how much I've changed?"* But the truth is, we're assuming people can instantly understand a version of us that has only just begun to emerge. We expect them to read a map we haven't even finished drawing. Because the hardest part is this: we don't yet fully know who we are.

We seem different because we are different.
Grief changes how we show up.
It changes what we tolerate, what we reach for, and what we can no longer carry.

This reorientation, this new way of being, is not a failure. It's the natural response to having loved deeply and lost deeply. It's the beginning of living from a truer place.

In the aftermath of loss, our attachments, the emotional glue that holds us together, start to shift. We might cling tighter to some, pull away from others, or retreat entirely. Not because we've stopped loving, but because our hearts are trying to find a safe place to land in a world that no longer feels safe. Grief scrambles our wiring. It makes intimacy both a balm and a trigger.

The truth is, love doesn't vanish when someone dies, or when a dream, a marriage, or a version of ourselves falls apart. It just changes form. And sometimes grief teaches us to move differently, as if we're learning a new dance while still stumbling, trying to right ourselves.

The Complicated Web We Weave

If grief had a relationship status, it would read: It's complicated.

Because once loss enters the picture, so does misunderstanding. The people who love us most can't always meet us where we are. Some rush in to fix it, armed with casseroles and platitudes. Others vanish, terrified of saying the wrong thing. We get angry. Then guilty for being angry. Then angry that we feel guilty.

Loss doesn't just shatter our hearts, it rewires our attachments. What once felt safe might now feel suffocating. What once comforted us can suddenly sting. Our nervous system is in survival mode, scanning for danger even in familiar faces. And that means our relationships, all of them, start shifting.

Psychologists call it attachment theory. I call it the beautiful mess of being human.

Some of us cling tighter (hello, anxious attachment), desperate for reassurance that love won't leave again. Others pull away, afraid that closeness will only bring more pain. Some do both: reaching out and retreating in the same breath. It's confusing, exhausting, and completely normal.

Grief teaches us a new language, one with strange grammar and untranslatable words. Sometimes all we can manage is a shrug, a sigh, or a quiet I don't know. But this new language, as awkward as it feels, is how we begin to reconnect with others and with ourselves. It's the slow process of relearning how to trust, to be held, to let someone see us when our hearts are still cracked open.

And maybe that's grace: not in the tidy, ribbon-wrapped way we were taught, but in the raw, real way love keeps showing up, even when we're not sure we know how to receive it.

What We Do to Survive

Depending on what kind of loss you've lived through and the chaos that surrounded it, your coping looks different. Some people collapse inward, some run, some organize closets at 2 a.m. For me, the only way I knew how to survive was *to do.* To move. To control what I could control, and to keep moving through what I couldn't.

I became what is called a "practical griever," the one who makes lists, cleans out closets, pays bills, and checks on everyone else while quietly falling apart inside. My safety became my emotional fortress of protection. Being in action gave me the illusion of safety. If I could just do the next thing, I didn't have to feel the enormity of what I'd lost. I told myself, "Keep going. Just keep moving." Because stopping meant sinking, and honestly,I really didn't have the faith that I would ever be able to resurface if I gave in.

What I didn't understand then was that all this "doing" was also a kind of language: my nervous system's way of saying, I'm not ready to sit in the stillness yet. Practical grief was how I kept functioning in a world that had stopped making sense.

The problem is, not everyone grieves that way. And that's where the emotional entanglements begin. When your way of surviving doesn't match someone else's way of hurting, misunderstandings multiply. One person wants to talk; the other wants to scrub the kitchen floor. One needs space; the other needs closeness. It's not wrong. It's just different dialects of the same brokenhearted language.

When Safety Shifts

The mismatch isn't just about coping styles; it's about how we relate to everything. Grief doesn't stop at the borders of an intimate relationship; it seeps into the way we move through the world. The places, people, and routines that once felt steady can suddenly feel foreign. The world tilts. What was safe before doesn't always feel safe after.

That was definitely my case. The life I had tried to build, the rhythms, the roles, even the spaces I used to find comfort in, no longer fit. I felt like a stranger in my own story. And that's one of the hardest parts of grief: realizing that safety, as you knew it, may not exist in the same way anymore.

So we go searching. Sometimes we look for safety in work, or busyness, or control. Sometimes we find it in people who mirror our brokenness, and sometimes we chase it in places that can't hold us. We're trying to locate ourselves in a world that's been rearranged, and that's no small task.

This is where many relationships strain. One person clings to the familiar, desperate to restore "before." The other has already crossed into the unrecognizable "after." It's not that love disappears; it's that the map changes, and no one gives us directions for how to find each other again.

But maybe that's what healing really is: not going back to the old safe places, if you were lucky enough to even know what that was, but learning to build new ones, slowly, piece by piece, as we learn to trust life again.

The Geography of Safety

I've thought a lot about what it really means to feel unsafe. It isn't just about danger in the physical sense: it's about not knowing where it's okay to be fully yourself anymore. When loss rips through your life, it doesn't just take what you love; it shakes your foundation. You wake up one day and realize that the inner coordinates that once guided you, who you are, who you trust, where you belong have literally become scrambled.

We can do the deep inner work: therapy, journaling, prayer, movement, and begin to find a sense of inner safety, that quiet place inside that whispers, You're okay right now. But building outer safety, with people, places, and community, is something else entirely. That takes risk. It takes discernment. And it takes time.

It's like waking up in a country where you don't speak the language and the landmarks are gone. Your family, your friends, even your neighborhood, all look the same on the outside, but feel totally unfamiliar. You wonder, can the people around me still see me? Can they handle who I've become? Sometimes the answer is yes. Other times, painfully, it's no.

That dissonance, between the world you once trusted and the new one you're trying to navigate, can slow healing. Because safety isn't just about feeling calm; it's about feeling seen. Without that, we start to armor up, shrink, and perform.

Healing asks for openness, but openness requires trust, and trust can feel like walking barefoot on broken glass after loss. For many of us, we say to ourselves emphatically. "Well, that's not going to happen."

And yet, in this messy and often confusing place is where grace quietly begins to rebuild us, helping us find new people, new places, and new rhythms that reflect the person we've become. Grace even brings us back to ourselves. It's not the same inner or outer landscape, but over time, it starts to feel like some semblance of home again, a different home, yes, but one that's built on truth, not illusion or false expectations.

The Inverted Search for Safety

Some people try to rebuild from the outside in. They move, change jobs, find new relationships, new routines: all in an effort to make life feel steady again. When your inner world feels like rubble, the outer world seems like the only thing you can control. Rearranging it gives the illusion that you're regaining ground.

After my first huge loss, the murder of my brother Matt, I did this too. I kept moving, changing my surroundings, boyfriends, setting new goals, and changing plans daily. It wasn't that I was running from pain; I was trying to outrun chaos. I believed if I could make the world around me safe, eventually my heart would catch up.

But the truth is, it doesn't work that way. You can build a fortress, but if your inner landscape is still trembling, the walls will always crack. Real safety, the kind that allows healing, has to start from within. It begins quietly, in the moments when you can breathe again without bracing for impact. It's not about controlling; it's about increasing your capacity to sit in the discomfort of loss. The capacity to hold what hurts without drowning in it.

Only then can you begin to let the outer world mirror that inner calm-through people who can meet you there, environments that feel nurturing, and experiences that support peace rather than chaos.

Grief flips the order of everything. It dismantles the illusion that we can build our way back to safety from the outside in. Healing asks us to do the often more difficult work of restoring our soul from the inside out, until our inner peace becomes the divine compass for the life we're creating from here.

The Fragile Work of Trust

If safety is the ground beneath us, trust is the bridge we build to step forward again. And after loss, that bridge feels shaky or even non-existent. The people we trusted to show up sometimes disappear. The ones we counted on to understand sometimes don't. And suddenly, the world that once felt familiar starts to feel unpredictable.

Trust is complicated after loss because it's often not about other people. Even though we find it easier to project the hurt onto others, it's about ourselves. Can I trust my own heart again? My instincts? My capacity to open and not break? Grief has a way of cracking open every illusion of control, and rebuilding trust means learning to live without any guarantees.

When I lost Will, I didn't just lose my son. I lost a certain trust in how life worked. I had always believed that if you loved with an open heart and did good, life would, at least occasionally, meet you halfway. But grief tore that map in two. I found myself questioning everything, from faith to fairness to my own ability to continue.

Trusting others after that felt like trying to hand someone a glass heart. What if they drop it? What if I do? So we hold back, test the waters, look for proof that it's safe to love again. But the truth is, trust doesn't return all at once. It rebuilds itself slowly, through consistent kindness, through people who don't look away, through the quiet knowing that even if it breaks again, we can survive it.

Relearning trust means allowing others to meet us where we are, not where we used to be. It's understanding that some will disappoint us, but others will surprise us with their capacity to hold space for our new, unpolished selves. It's the slow, deliberate act of unclenching the heart, not because we're naïve, but because we're brave.

And maybe that's what grace really looks like in this stage of the journey: not blind faith that everything will be okay, but a tender willingness to believe that love, even after all it's taken, still has something to give.

Grace: The Gentle Teacher of Trust

Grace doesn't rush. It doesn't demand that we trust again before we're ready. It simply waits, soft but steady, beside our fear. Grace whispers, *you can open a little more now*, and when we do, it meets us there. It still surprises me with its impact and glory.

It shows up in the friend who keeps checking in, even when we don't answer. In the small moments we laugh again without guilt. In the stillness when we realize that the ache in our chest isn't quite as sharp as before. Grace is the gap between closing and reopening, where the heart remembers it can love again, even if it loves differently.

For me, grace looked like letting myself be a raw and vulnerable human again, not polished and tidy, not perfect, but fully present. It was learning that I could hold grief in one hand and gratitude in the other. That trust didn't mean pretending I wasn't afraid; it meant stepping forward with the fear and choosing to connect with others anyway, even through shaking knees and a timid heart.

We think healing means putting the pieces back where they were. But grace teaches us that healing is about creating something new from what remains. It's not about forgetting or replacing what was lost: it's about learning to live fully in the presence of both love and loss.

Reflection: Love in Motion

Grief changes how we love. It rewrites our attachments, our sense of safety, and our capacity to trust. It's disorienting and exhausting, like trying to walk along a tightrope. But if we stay with it, if we keep listening for grace in the middle of the mess, something begins to shift in our hearts.

We start to recognize that love itself was never the problem. The ache we feel is proof that love worked. It left an imprint deep enough to rearrange us. And while it's tempting to protect our hearts forever, what grief ultimately asks of us is courage, the courage to love again- that raw, messy kind of love, not all "neat and tidy," but refreshingly new.

And even here on the grief journey, in the tangled, complicated, beautiful aftermath, love remains the thread that leads us home.

Reflection Questions

1. How has loss changed the way you connect with others, or with yourself?

2. What does "safety" mean to you now, and where do you feel it most (or least) in your life?

3. In what ways have your relationships shifted since your loss? Who has stayed, who has drifted, and how has that shaped you?

4. What would rebuilding trust, with yourself or another, look like right now, even in small steps?

5. Where do you sense grace showing up quietly in your healing, even when it's hard to see?

6. What new language of love are you learning to speak, one that honors both your grief and your growth?

Chapter 13

The Alchemy of Grace

Sometimes grace begins as something so small you could almost overlook it: a deep sigh you didn't know you needed, a moment that doesn't hit quite as hard, a mustard seed of hope settling somewhere in your chest.

And sometimes God's grace doesn't arrive gently at all.
Sometimes it swoops in, sudden, unexpected, cutting through the heaviness before you even understand what's happening.
A stranger smiling at you in the grocery store.
A single leaf floating down as you grab the mail from the mailbox.
A puppy licks your face.
And for a second, the grip around your heart loosens, just enough to feel it.

Not because the grief is gone. Not because anything is fixed. But because grace meets us in ways we don't expect.

Sometimes God's grace brings deep, full-body laughter that surprises you.
Sometimes it brings tears that move freely, remembering what was beautiful and what was lost.
Sometimes it sweeps over you in a wave of awe or gratitude so unexpected you almost don't know what to do with it.

Grace reminds you that you are still alive, that your life still matters, that your heart hasn't stopped trying to belong here.

This is the messy middle where grief and grace overlap.
Where nothing is resolved, and everything is raw, and yet something inside you responds, a small shift, a quiet recognition, a reminder that your story isn't over.

God's grace doesn't pull you out of the mess. It meets you *inside* it, right where you're standing, right where it hurts, right where something new is trying to break through.

Client Story- Julie: Making Space for Grief and Grace

One of my clients, Julie, came to me after losing her husband. She told me, "I just want to stop crying." We sat quietly, and then I told her gently, "You don't need to stop. The tears are evidence of your love."

Together, we created simple practices: walks outside, small routines, honest conversations not to fix her pain, but to give it space to breathe, and heal. Over time, she began to notice things again: the feel of her dog's fur under her hand, the warmth of coffee in the morning, the sound of her own laughter catching her by surprise. None of it erased the loss. But it reminded her that grace hadn't gone anywhere. It was just waiting for her to hear the whisper- to let it in.

That's the alchemy: the slow transformation of unbearable pain into a quieter kind of strength: acceptance for what is. Acceptance doesn't mean you are done, it's time to move on. It means sitting in the present and feeling *what is*.

Faith as Surrender

I used to think faith meant being certain, believing that everything would eventually make sense. Now I see faith very differently. Grief has been a great teacher.

I realize now that faith isn't about control. It's saying, I don't understand this, but I'm willing to stay open anyway. It's trusting that God has me, that I will find the way if I just let go of control, of being right. This faith is not some form of blind optimism; it's courage.

It's choosing to believe that love and meaning can coexist with heartbreak, that light and darkness are both part of the same story. Grace works hand in hand with that kind of faith. It doesn't require explanations or tidy conclusions. It just asks you to breathe and take one small step toward life again, even if your hands are still shaking and your heart is racing.

Kate McKay

Grace in the Messy Middle

Grace doesn't rush in to fix what hurts. It meets you right where you are. Sometimes it arrives quietly, almost unnoticed. Other times it moves fast and unexpected, breaking through the heaviness before you can explain it. Grace doesn't wait for your life to be neat or steady, it steps into the mess with you, steadying you one breath at a time.

Healing isn't something to conquer; it's about allowing: our willingness to feel what's real without judging it. It's giving your emotions room to move through you, not locking them behind the door marked "strong and impenetrable" or "Been there, done that."

Grace does not show up at the end of grief. It's the thread that runs through it, often unseen, quietly weaving its way into our pain, fluid enough to hold us when everything else unravels. You may still feel raw, angry, disoriented. That's okay. Grace doesn't wait for composure, it meets you exactly where you are.

It lives in the middle of the mess: in the laughter that feels strange at first, in the conversations that bring both tears and relief, in the quiet mornings when you realize that even with the ache, you're still here. Grief doesn't get wrapped up with a bow. It becomes part of who you are, a tender scar that tells the truth about love.

Grace doesn't demand that you "move on." It helps you move with what's real, learning to live fully while carrying what remains. And that's the alchemy: the subtle, sacred shift that turns survival into living. You don't have to prove anything to deserve peace.

Grace is the invisible elixir that begins transforming loss into meaning, heartbreak into humility, and suffering into a deeper kind of love. It walks alongside you, right here, right now, calling your name.

Reflection Questions

1. Where do you notice grace showing up in the middle of your own mess right now, even in small, unexpected ways?

2. What emotions are asking for space to move through you, rather than being held behind the door marked "strong and impenetrable"?

3. How might it feel to let grace walk with you: not at the end of your grief, but right here, right now, calling your name?

Chapter 14

The Courage to Receive Help

There's a certain kind of exhaustion that comes after loss, not just the physical kind, but also the kind that seeps into your bones. You try to keep going, but everything takes more effort than it should. You tell yourself, I've got this. You've done it before. You know how to manage, hold it together, and make sure everyone else is okay.

Grief is like a storm that blows through your life and shakes everything you thought you could count on. It strips away the illusion that we can heal alone.

For a long time, I tried. I told myself I just needed to push through it, stay organized, manage the logistics, and take care of what needed to be done. You know: the usual plan for fixing a shattered heart. It was familiar terrain: survival mode.

People would look at me and say, "You're so strong, Kate. You're such an inspiration."

And I knew they meant well; it was their way of offering comfort. But after a while, those words started to feel like a prison. Because when you're praised for strength, you start to believe that's the only version of yourself people will accept. You learn to swallow the sob, to straighten your back, to hide the collapse that wants to be expressed that lies coiled within you.

And yet, real healing requires the very thing "strength" doesn't allow: letting yourself be held, to be witnessed.

It took me years to discover that I needed safe connection with people I trusted to be there for me, not just the people I hired. It took me years to ask for help at all. Sure, I hired a therapist and a coach. Hiring professionals was the easier choice. But leaning on anyone else? Not a chance.

Surviving, managing, and holding it all together while others fell apart around me had been a lifelong theme. But when the silence finally came, I realized something I'd spent decades avoiding: soul-level healing wouldn't happen until I stopped being the strong one and finally asked for support. I had to learn, almost like an infant, how to receive, how to be held, how to take in loving support without shame. And to be honest, even today, I'm still more like a toddler inches from a tantrum than someone calmly cooperating with nap time.

We all have lessons grief teaches us. Mine was to let down the drawbridge and be courageous enough to let people in, without feeling like I was going to drown.

This has been one of the hardest lessons of all.

Why Receiving Help Feels So Hard

It took me a long time to understand why receiving felt so impossible. I had convinced myself I was evolved, self-aware, spiritually mature- pick your newest and trendiest term. I thought I was doing all the "right" things: staying busy, staying helpful, staying strong. In fact, I was praised for all of these things. What I didn't realize was that all I was doing was keeping me from receiving grace.

I was running on adrenaline and grit. ADHD-fueled momentum. Protein shakes. The next success. The next fitness competition. The next mountain to climb. I mistook non-stop motion for strength, when, really, it was my favorite form of escape.

But the breaking didn't come right away. It came much later, when I finally stopped running, sat down, and … stayed. When I stopped distracting myself and grief rushed in like a tidal wave. In the loneliness, in the tears, in the whispered *I can't do this alone*, that's when grace finally swooped in to my rescue.

That moment, the one that cracked me open, is why I wrote this book. Because healing didn't begin in the hustle, the conquering, or the next big goal. It began when I finally stayed still long enough to receive.

It didn't feel graceful at first. It felt like unraveling: like every defense I'd built suddenly had nothing left to lean on. But that's the thing about grace: it doesn't ask you to be impressive; it asks you to be honest. It shows up in the places you've avoided, waiting for the moment you're willing to be seen.

For me, that shift began when I finally let people in, trusting breath at a time. Letting myself be witnessed in my pain, without trying to fix or perform, softened something in me I didn't even know had hardened. That's where I began to feel God meeting me too, apparently unruffled by my mess. It was the birth of a different kind of strength, the kind that is only allowed to grow when you allow yourself to be fully and vulnerably seen.

A Client's Story- Marissa: Learning to Let People In

One of my clients, Marissa, came to me after a string of losses, a divorce, the death of her father, and the unraveling of a business she'd built from the ground up. She was deep in grief, stressed and exhausted.

She said, "I'm tired of being the strong one. But I don't know how to stop." We talked about control and how it can be both a shield and a cage. Marissa wasn't afraid of pain; she was afraid of being seen in it.

Together, we practiced small acts of allowing: Saying yes to a friend's offer to help her clean out her dad's place, joining a group to deal with her grief and loss, accepting a compliment instead of deflecting it. It was awkward at first, but over time, she learned that letting people help, while seeing her not all put together, and it didn't mean she was falling apart. It meant she was opening to love in a new form.

That's the sweet courage of receiving: the willingness to be cared for when you've never trusted that you would be cared for in return.

Letting People Be Part of the Process

Healing happens in community, not isolation. Sometimes that community looks like friends who show up and stay. Sometimes it's a therapist, pastor, or coach, someone who can hold space when the people closest to you can't. And sometimes it's a stranger whose unexpected kindness reminds you that the world is still capable of tenderness.

But the real turning point isn't *who* shows up. It's your willingness to let them. Your willingness to risk being open, even when you're not sure your needs will be met. Your willingness to be honest instead of polished, seen instead of guarded. That kind of vulnerability can feel terrifying, like stepping out without any guarantees. But that's where grace begins: right in the moment you choose to open anyway.

Faith in People, Faith in Love

Letting others help you is a form of faith. It's saying, *I believe love still exists, even here.* It's trusting that vulnerability won't drown you, but actually save you. The bravest thing you can do after loss is to stay open to love, to risk connection, even when your heart feels like it can't trust anyone, not even yourself..

Because love is what shaped you. And it's what will carry you through.

But here's the hard truth: loss changes you. You don't walk through fire and come out the same. Some people can't handle the new you, the depth, the rawness, the truth that grief leaves behind. They may pull away, say the wrong thing, or disappear entirely. That's another kind of loss: one that compounds the pain.

It's tempting to close off, to decide you're safer alone. But isolation is not protection; it's paralysis. The work of healing is learning to discern who can meet you where you are now, and to trust that the right people will stay.

Healing doesn't happen because you have it all figured out.
It happens when you finally say, *I can't do this alone.*
That's not surrender. That's resurrection.

Discernment: Learning Who Can Hold Your Heart

Discernment isn't judgmental: I call it sacred clarity. It's the quiet knowing that comes when you stop chasing who left and start honoring who stayed. It's how you begin to tell the difference between people who comfort your wounds and those who keep reopening them. Discernment helps you rebuild trust, not all at once, but piece by piece, with the ones who can meet your truth with tenderness.

But here's what no one tells you: discernment isn't something you wake up magically knowing how to do. Most of us weren't taught it, especially if we grew up being praised for being "strong," "helpful," "resilient," or "easygoing." We were taught to give, to care, to show up, not to notice how our body reacts when someone steps into our emotional space. Not to question whether someone has earned access to our hearts.

And let's be honest, discernment gets a lot more complicated when you've lived through rejection, betrayal, or heartbreak. When you've been left to pick up the pieces alone. When you've convinced yourself you can handle everything without needing anyone. Discernment in those seasons isn't just wisdom, it's survival. It's learning to trust again, slowly. Carefully. Without abandoning yourself in the process.

Discernment isn't about closing your heart; it's about protecting the sacred. It's the courage to ask, *Who has earned the right to hear my pain? Who has shown they can hold my truth without dropping it? Who can sit with me instead of trying to fix, control, or judge me?*

And here's the real shift: grace doesn't only come through the presence of the right people, grace comes through your willingness to let those people in, even though it feels risky, even though your whole body might still brace for disappointment. Discernment is trusting yourself enough to open the door a little and see what happens.

You can learn this. You can strengthen this. And you can practice it in a way that honors your heart, your healing, and your story.

Steps to Help with Discernment

1. **Pause Before You Reach Out.**
   When your heart aches for connection, take a moment to breathe before you text, call, or confide. Not everyone has earned a front-row seat to your healing. That pause isn't about withholding love, it's about honoring your energy and choosing the right person to share your heart with.
2. **Notice How Your Body Feels.**
   Your body holds clues you've probably been taught to ignore. Some people make your shoulders drop and your breath deepen; others make your chest tighten. Your nervous system reacts faster than your logic ever will. Your body knows who feels safe- tune in.
3. **Watch for Reciprocity.**
   Healthy love flows both ways. Notice who asks about *you*, who remembers the small things, who shows up without fixing or fleeing. Real compassion doesn't rush you to be "okay"; it meets you where you are. You are worthy of receiving support and care.
4. **Speak with Loving Directness**
   Grief can sharpen our edges. When you need to express a boundary or truth, let it come from ca alm, not defensive, place "I'm not ready for that conversation yet" or "I need some space right now" are holy sentences.
5. **Bless and Release.**
   Some relationships won't survive your transformation and there's grace in that too. Bless them silently and let them go. Every ending makes room for a new beginning that aligns with who you are becoming.
6. **Stay Open to Surprise.**
   Grace loves to work through unexpected people: a kind stranger, a new friend, a conversation that infuses hope in your soul. Stay open. The heart, once cracked, becomes a doorway for more goodness to enter, if you choose.

You don't have to carry everything by yourself. Sometimes grace wears a human face, a friend, a stranger, a pet, a hand reaching toward you. Let it in. You were never meant to do this alone.

Reflection Questions

1. When have you found yourself resisting help and what was underneath that resistance?

2. Who has offered you kindness that you quietly turned away from?

3. What would it feel like to let your own drawbridge down, even just an inch?

Chapter 15

Forgiveness, Release and What Comes After

Life has a way of splitting itself in two.
Before the loss. After the loss.

When grief arrives, it doesn't ask permission. It barges in and rearranges everything you thought you knew. Sometimes it's the death of someone you love. Sometimes it's betrayal, a friendship that quietly disappears, a diagnosis you never saw coming, or a dream that collapses in a heap at your feet.

However it shows up, grief leaves a hollow ache, where words can't quite explain.

And it's not just sadness: it's a rewiring of who we are.
The air feels heavier. The world keeps moving, but you are no longer turning in the same way. Time speeds up, then moves like molasses, especially as you lie in bed in the dark. Colors dull. Laughter feels foreign. Yet somehow, you keep breathing. That's the first miracle: that your breath still finds you and moves through you.

Grief simplifies life. It strips away the noise and reveals what is sacred. And slowly, if you let it, a quiet kind of grace begins to move beneath the rubble.

When my son Will died, a part of me died too. I am not going to sugar-coat this one. There was no tidy way through the pain; only the choice to keep showing up for the day in front of me. And there were many mornings, when I would look in the mirror and whisper to myself through tears, "*Just keep swimming, Kate.*"

Remember the movie *Finding Nemo*? I've always loved that little clownfish. Nemo had one tiny, crooked fin, and it never stopped him from showing up fully and enthusiastically, no matter what he was up against. His "defect" didn't make him less than: it made him real because don't we all feel a bit broken in some way? Nemo was living proof that courage has nothing to do with perfection or having it all together. He just kept going, even when the current was way stronger than he was.

When I came across that movie again after my son Will died, it hit me on a whole different level. What once felt like a simple story suddenly held the language of survival, grit, and hope.

Aren't we all like Nemo in our own way, navigating our days with some part of us that no longer works the way it once did, swimming through loss, fear, or uncertainty? And yet, somehow, we keep going. Some days gracefully, some days floating half mast on the surface, but always and miraculously onward.

Because healing is not about fixing what is broken. It is about clinging to the mustard seed of faith; faith that every small movement counts, that God or whatever life force you believe in meets you in the deep, even when you cannot see the shore.

The Weight of What-Ifs

Forgiveness shows up in every kind of loss. It isn't only about people who have passed—it's about relationships that ended before we were ready, choices we can't undo, seasons we outgrew, and the versions of ourselves we've had to leave behind. Loss doesn't just take something from us; it often hands us a pile of questions we never asked for.

The mind loves to replay what cannot be changed:
What if I had said something sooner?
What if I had stayed?
What if I had seen it coming?
Those thoughts can loop endlessly, and they carry a weight that settles into the body, the breath, the spirit.

Forgiveness is not denial. It's not pretending the pain didn't matter or rushing toward meaning before the wound has been acknowledged. It's an internal, heart-based decision to stop fighting the past and to stop rehearsing the story that holds you captive.

Forgiveness does not let anyone off the hook. It gives you your life back from the moment that hurt you. It's the slow un-clenching of the fist, the exhale that follows a long-held tension. It's the moment you finally admit, *I cannot carry this alone,* and you surrender, and perhaps hand the heaviest parts over to God, trusting that He can hold what broke you and guide you into what's next.

Lessons in Forgiveness

When my brother Matt was killed in 1987, forgiveness stopped being an idea and became something I had to live through. My family responded in a way that soothed me at the time. Maybe it was some Catholic thing, but there was no rage, no thirst for revenge,
just grief.
We knew no amount of fury would bring him back.

The loss ripped through us, rearranging everything. Each of us coped differently: some through work, others through silence, and for a few, through the slow escape of alcohol or drugs.

For me, grief became something practical- cleaning out his room, showing up to pre-trial hearings, making calls I could barely get through, shuffling my time between my mom and dad, who were already separated and then divorced soon after

I can still see my mother sitting in her rocker, numb, holding the phone after the call from the Connecticut police. Outside, the Red Sox were preparing for a doubleheader at Fenway, and pigeons were cooing in the courtyard. The world kept moving, unaware that ours had just stopped.

And then my father, the sound of his keys hitting the floor when I told him what happened to his son. That rattling sound still lives in me.

I felt bad for me, sure, but what about my mom and dad? I kept saying to myself and others, not giving myself grace to grieve the intense loss of my buddy, only 18 months younger than me.

Grief stripped bare is profound sadness. It changes your DNA. It leaves you raw and exposed, unsure how to keep moving when the world has tilted off its axis.

And yet somehow, we did move forward. Certainly not gracefully, just one messy step at a time.

Looking back now, I see that my family's lack of vengeance was not detachment; it was a kind of mercy. Forgiveness did not come because we were that evolved; it came because anger was too heavy for us , as a family, to carry. We chose, consciously or not, to let God hold what we could not.

That experience shaped the way I see forgiveness.
It is not tidy or noble. It is grace in action.
It is saying, *I will not let this darkness be the whole story.*
It is the slow work of trusting that God can redeem even this, that grace can meet us in the places we never wanted to go.

Reflection Questions

1. Where in your life have you held onto anger or blame because it felt safer than touching the grief underneath? What might soften in you if you allowed the sadness, not the rage, to speak first?

2. When you think about forgiveness, not the pretty, polished version, but the fragile, relentless work of continuing, what part of your story still feels too heavy to carry alone? Who or what might you allow to shoulder a piece of it with you?

3. How has loss reshaped your inner landscape, your faith, your sense of self, your worldview, and where do you sense grace slowly meeting you in the places you once believed were beyond healing?

4. If you could speak to the grief, what would you say? What does your heart need to hear?

Chapter 16

Learning to Live with What Remains

No one tells you what comes after grief. We expect some kind of finish line, but there isn't one. What comes after isn't closure: it's learning to allow what's here now. It's learning to live with what remains and finding small, honest ways to rebuild a life inside it.

You might never "move on," but you *can* move with. Over time, the weight shifts. You begin to carry your loss differently. Tiny moments of light slip back in, a laugh that surprises you, a second where your shoulders drop, a quiet sense of appreciation you didn't think you'd feel again. And you might even feel pangs of guilt, like, *How can I be feeling better?* That's normal too. Grief doesn't leave; it makes room for the peace to settle back in.

I remember standing in the grocery store once when I apparently, in my usual ADHD whoopsie fashion, dropped a glove. A stranger tapped me on the shoulder and handed it back. Tears filled my eyes, not from heartbreak, but from gratitude. This tiny, ordinary moment cracked something open in me. I think he thought I was crazy, but I just couldn't hold back the simple joy I felt in my heart. It reminded me that grace doesn't always arrive in big revelations. Sometimes it just shows up through simple human kindness.

Healing isn't about replacing what's gone; it's about making space for what's still alive. Love doesn't disappear; it just changes form. It keeps evolving right alongside you. I know that may be hard to believe, but I promise you, it's true.

And slowly, so slowly you barely notice it at first, the landscape of your heart starts to shift. You breathe a little deeper. You laugh a little easier. You find yourself able to feel joy again, small at first, then stronger. We fight acceptance with everything we've got, convinced that surrender means letting go of the person we lost. But eventually, there comes a moment when you raise the white flag, not in defeat, but in salty-sweet acceptance. In honesty. In the simple recognition that *this is where I am now. This is who I am now. Here I am.*

And strangely, that is where a greater sense of peace begins: not in forgetting what was, but in learning to live with what remains.

A Client's Story- Paul: The Release

One of my clients, Paul, came to me after a painful breakup of his marriage that left him questioning everything: his worth, his choices, even his identity as a man. He said, "I do not know who I am without her. I just want to make sense of it."

What he really yearned for was peace. But peace does not come from understanding where we messed up, or they messed up, or whatever the scenario may be; it comes from releasing the attachment to the idea that we can control the outcome: mto buffer ourselves from the pain of loss.

We worked not to erase the pain, but to listen to it. He began to see that his guilt was simply love with nowhere to go. Instead of trying to *move on,* we practiced letting love move *through* him- in how he showed up for his kids, in his friendships, in the work that began calling him again.

Over time, the grip loosened. The self-blame began to fade. Paul could look at the relationship not as a failure but as something sacred that had run its course and taught him how deeply he could love.

That is release.
Not letting go of love, but letting go of punishment and permitting yourself to feel joy once again. We all deserve that sense of freedom. Me. You. And Paul.

Grace for What Comes After

Forgiveness and release aren't really about "closure."
They're about giving ourselves some room, room in our lives and in our healing.
Room to breathe again.
Room for the fog to finally start lifting.
Room to let life move forward without piling a bunch of unrealistic expectations on our shoulders.

Grace is woven through all of that.

Grace brings us right back into the present moment.
It reminds us who we are, and who God is.
It has this way of humbling us and strengthening us at the same time … steadying our feet while opening our hearts to what's still here.

And grace helps us stop resisting what's real, so we can start making meaning out of what remains.
It lets us honor the love that was without getting swallowed by the loss.

It keeps whispering: *You're not walking this alone.*

Some days, the ache will land just as sharply as it always has.
Other days, laughter will sneak up on you and catch you by surprise.

That's not forgetting.
That's remembering with a little more peace and a little more room to breathe.
That's grace doing what grace does, meeting you exactly where you are and nudging you forward, one honest step at a time.

Reflection

1. What kind of loss are you carrying right now—a person, a relationship, a dream, or a piece of who you used to be?

2. Which "what-ifs" keep tugging at you, and what might it look like to release even one of them today?

3. How could forgiveness, especially of yourself, create a little more room for grace in your life?

You will not return to who you were before. But you can keep swimming, tender, wiser, alive. That is the quiet miracle of forgiveness and release: it turns love into something that can breathe again.

The Practice of Forgiveness: 7 Compassionate Steps

Forgiveness is not a single moment. It's a process, a loosening, a softening, a slow unclenching of the places that grief and loss have tightened. It asks for willingness, not perfection. It is a practice, a return, a gentle choosing again and again.

Here are the steps I've seen shape real healing in my own life and in the lives of the people I walk beside.

1. Acknowledge the Hurt Fully and Honestly

Forgiveness begins with truth-telling. You cannot heal what you refuse to name.
Acknowledge what happened, how it changed you, what it cost you, and the impact it had on your sense of safety, worth, or identity.

This step isn't about blame.
It's about giving your pain the dignity of being seen.

2. Allow Yourself to Feel What You Feel

Forgiveness isn't possible if you bypass your emotions.
The sadness, the anger, the disappointment, the shock, they all need space to move through you.

Your feelings aren't wrong or inconvenient.
They are your heart's evidence that this mattered.
Feeling them is not indulgence, it's honesty.

3. Separate the Wound From Your Worth

Pain has a way of whispering lies about who you are.
This step is about reclaiming yourself.

What happened is part of your story,
but it is not your identity.
You are not the betrayal, the harm, or the abandonment. You are the one who lived through it.

Forgiveness begins with remembering who you are.

4. Release What Isn't Yours to Carry

Forgiveness is less about the other person and more about freeing *yourself* from the emotional weight that doesn't belong to you.

The resentment, the bitterness, the spiraling what-ifs: these can keep your heart trapped in yesterday.

Releasing doesn't mean excusing.
It means refusing to let the pain define your future.

5. Invite God (or Grace) Into the Places Too Heavy to Hold Alone

There will be moments when softening feels impossible.
This is where grace steps in.

Forgiveness asks for a strength beyond our own- a divine tenderness that meets us right where we are.
You don't forgive because you're more evolved.
You forgive because the weight is too heavy to carry by yourself.

Let grace hold what you cannot.

6. Honor Your Boundaries and Your Freedom to Choose What Comes Next

Forgiveness and relationships are separate choices.
You can forgive someone and still choose whether you want to continue the relationship … or not.
You get to redefine what works for you, what doesn't, and what kind of connection (if any) honors your emotional and spiritual well-being.

Boundaries aren't punishment.
They're clear.
They're self-respect in action.

Forgiveness may soften your heart, but boundaries protect it. Choosing distance doesn't make you unkind. It makes you wise.

7. Choose Meaning: The Step That Transforms the Wound

Meaning doesn't erase the loss.
It gives the loss direction.
It's the quiet, sacred shift from *"Why did this happen?"* to *"What now?"*

Meaning is the stage David Kessler expanded on in his book ***Finding Meaning: The Sixth Stage of Grief,*** the place where the heart begins to integrate grief into a deeper purpose.

It asks:
What can grow from this pain?
Who am I becoming because of what I've lived through?
How can I carry the love forward without carrying the wound with it?

Meaning is where forgiveness becomes freedom.

Forgiveness doesn't rewrite what happened.
It writes who you become next.

Chapter Gratitude and Acceptance: The Doorway to Healing

"Deep calls to deep in the roar of your waterfalls; all your waves and breakers have swept over me."
– Psalm 42:7

There's a moment in every grief journey when you stop asking, *"Why did this happen?"* and begin to whisper, *"Now what?"* It's not a moment of defeat. It's the moment the heart begins to shift from survival to transformation.

Gratitude and acceptance aren't the prizes you receive at the end of grief. They're the quiet companions that walk beside you as you slowly rebuild a life in the shadow of what you've lost. They don't demand perfection or positivity. They simply ask for honesty and presence.

Gratitude doesn't erase pain; it helps it become more bearable.
It softens the sharp edges just enough for you to take the next breath, the next step, the next small act of living. It reminds you that even in the darkest seasons, there are still glimmers: a kind word, a sunset, a memory that makes you smile despite yourself.

Acceptance is trickier.
We like to imagine acceptance as a peaceful moment of clarity, but that's rarely how it happens. Most of us arrive at acceptance kicking and screaming, resisting it with everything we have. We fear that if we accept what happened, we're somehow agreeing to it, or worse, that accepting the loss means letting go of the love.

But acceptance is not forgetting.
It is not abandoning the memory.
It is not saying the pain didn't matter or the love wasn't real.

Acceptance is allowing, allowing the truth of what was, the reality of what is, and the continued presence of love that still lives inside you. It's the slow, reluctant shift from fighting reality to learning how to live with it. Not neatly, not gracefully, and certainly not all at once, but with a grounded courage that grows over time.

Gratitude steadies the heart.
Acceptance steadies the soul.
Together, they make room for healing to begin its quiet work.

Client Story- Kathy's Journey to Acceptance and Holy Surrender

My friend Kathy taught me more about acceptance than any book, therapist, or spiritual teacher ever could. When she was diagnosed with cancer, everyone around her, especially her devoted husband, wanted her to "fight."
To battle.
To push.
To go to war, to defeat the cancer. This language is common when you hear people talk of cancer.

But Kathy made a different choice.
She decided she wasn't going to fight cancer.
She wasn't going to battle it, blame it, or treat her body like an enemy.

Instead, she said,
"I'm going to meet this with all the faith I have."

She believed, with a steady clarity, that acceptance wasn't giving up; it was turning toward healing in a different form. Kathy held onto what she called *holy hope*: the kind that doesn't demand outcomes but stays open to grace in whatever way it comes.

Her family, especially her husband, struggled with her approach. They wanted action, effort, something to push against. But Kathy felt called to something else, something quieter and braver. She trusted that healing wasn't always about defeating an illness … sometimes healing is the way you choose to live in the middle of it.

Near the end of her life, I went to visit her.
She was resting in bed in the living room, the room dim and soft. I climbed in beside her, the way you do when someone you love is nearing a threshold too sacred to name.

The peace around her was unlike anything I've ever felt.
It wasn't resignation.
It wasn't giving up.
It was a holiness, an unmistakable presence of Love stripped bare, the kind that fills a room and silences every fear, if you are willing to step into it.

Lying next to her, I felt as though I were in the presence of an angel. It took my breath away. The quiet, the gentleness in her voice. It felt like she had already begun slipping into a kind of peace most of us never experience in this lifetime.

And in my heart, she is still that:
an angel,
a teacher,
a living embodiment of what acceptance can look like when it is joined with faith.

Kathy didn't lose to cancer.
She met it.
She walked with it.
She accepted what was happening while still holding onto God, hope, and love with both hands.

Her life, and her peaceful passing, remind me that acceptance isn't weakness.
It is courage.
It is trust.
It is choosing to be held by something larger than fear.

A few nights before my friend Kathy died, I had an experience I still struggle to fully describe. I was asleep and suddenly awakened by the vivid image of a small, fairy-like presence, rolling gently onto its side. So vivid that I bolted upright in bed and said out loud:

"Kathy is gone."

I reached for my phone, convinced I had seen a text with the news. I wrote to her husband expressing my sorrow. Later, he called and asked, "How did you know she died?"

"You texted me," I said.

"No," he told me. "I didn't. No one knew yet."

I checked. There was no text.
I told him about the little fairy rolling onto its side, how real it felt.

He didn't say much then, only that he was baffled.

A couple of weeks later, he invited me over for tea. He sat me down and said, "Tell me again what you saw." So I did, the fairy-like presence rolling onto its side, how certain I was that Kathy had passed.

He listened quietly, not emotional, just attentive. And then he said:

"After she died, the doula helped me bathe her. And then, following the doula's instructions … we turned her onto her side."

John explained how the doula had said that just as we enter the world curled like an infant in the womb, it is meaningful to return to that posture in death.

We both sat in the awe of the moment.

Our hearts were heavy in the shared grief, yet there was a peaceful stillness between us, an unspoken understanding that the Holy Spirit had moved through both of us.

There are some moments in life that logic alone cannot hold.
Moments where the veil feels thin.
Moments where love makes itself known in ways that bypass every rational pathway.

In her dying, Kathy left me a final gift: a reminder that acceptance isn't giving up, it's leaning into something larger, something truer.

Acceptance is the quiet courage to let love carry you into whatever comes next.
And sometimes, if we are paying attention, love sends a sign to let us know it has arrived.

The Alchemy of Gratitude

At first, practicing gratitude can feel impossible, even insulting. How can we be grateful when something or someone we love is gone?

But over time, gratitude changes form. It stops being a list and becomes a living language, the way our hearts speak to what remains.

Gratitude is how we honor the love that shaped us. It's how we begin to reclaim beauty, even in brokenness.

When we can whisper "thank you" not because everything is okay, but because love existed at all, we begin to touch grace. That quiet shift opens a door in the heart, one that leads us toward peace, even when life still hurts.

Acceptance: The Practice of Allowing

Acceptance is not surrender. It's not saying, "I'm fine." It's saying, "I'm willing to be with what is."

The process of acceptance has no timeline. It unfolds in its own rhythm, like tides, like seasons, like breath.

Some days we feel strong and clear; the next, we're pulled under again. That's not regression, that's real healing. It's messy, unpredictable, and many days, just downright hard.

Acceptance asks for courage, not control. It invites us to stop fighting the story and start living within it, not as victims of what happened, but as witnesses to how love continues to move through us, one breath at a time.

Survivor's Guilt and the Weight of Why

For many, acceptance is blocked by a haunting question: Why them and not me? Why this loss and not another?

Survivor's guilt can show up in many ways, the parent who outlives a child, the friend who walks away from the accident, the woman who survives the illness when another doesn't, or the one who leaves a broken relationship and wonders if they could have tried harder.

We replay the moment, bargaining with fate. But guilt is not love, it's love tangled with pain.

True love wants us to live. To carry the memory, the lesson, the meaning forward, not as a burden, but as a blessing.

I remember working with a woman named Laura. Her husband had died suddenly after forty years of marriage. When she first came to me, she sat across from me, holding herself so tightly I could almost feel the ache in her bones. She didn't want advice. She didn't need tools. She needed to be seen.

So we didn't start with a plan.

We started with witnessing.

I created a space where her grief could speak freely, where she didn't have to hold it together for anyone. There were long pauses and moments of quiet where the only thing between us was the sound of her tears. Sometimes I said nothing. Sometimes all I said was, "I see you."

Weeks passed like that, sacred conversations filled with the raw truth of missing him. Then one day, she looked up and whispered, "I feel guilty for still being here. It feels wrong to live when he can't."

That's when we began to talk about guilt, how sometimes it's just love, disguised as suffering. How it's the heart's way of keeping someone close. I asked her gently, "If he could sit here beside you right now, what would he want for you?"

She paused. Her voice shook.

"He'd want me to laugh again," she said. "He always said my laugh could fill a room."

"That's where we'll start," I told her. "Not by forgetting him, but by remembering him through the sound of your laughter."

It took months, but slowly, life began to move through her again. A walk with friends. Volunteering at the garden he used to tend. The day she laughed during one of our calls, really laughed, she covered her mouth and started crying. "I thought if I laughed, I'd lose him," she said. "But I think he's here at this moment."

In that moment, Laura began to shift from surviving her loss to allowing life to return, a gentle reminder that even in the depth of grief, we still have the power to choose presence, to remember the love that was and still remains.

The work of healing is not to justify why we survived, but to honor that we did, and to use that breath, that heartbeat, that continued life as a tribute to what was lost.

Survival is not selfishness. It's a sacred continuation.

The Trap of Victim Consciousness

After the Holocaust, people who survived did not all go on to live in the same way. Survival alone didn't determine how life would feel afterward. Some continued with the curtains drawn, alive, functioning, doing what was required, but with their inner world shattered. Their nervous systems stayed on alert. Their hearts stayed cautious. Given what they had endured, this made complete sense. It wasn't a weakness. It was a way of staying safe in a world that had proven itself dangerous.

Others, impossibly, found ways to pull the curtains open.

Not because their suffering was smaller or their losses fewer. Many had lost everything: families, homes, a sense of order, even faith itself. And still, over time, some chose not to let what happened become the only story they lived inside of. They carried grief and memory with them, but they also found ways to love again, to build something meaningful, to laugh, to contribute, to stay connected to life. Not by forgetting what happened, but by, in some way, integrating it.

Curtains down or curtains up was never about character or virtue. It wasn't about who was "stronger." It was about how each person's inner world responded to trauma, timing, support, and the slow, uneven process of meaning-making.

This matters when we talk about grief.

When grief isn't given space to be acknowledged, it can quietly harden into a kind of victim consciousness, not as a choice, but as protection. We project the pain outside of us because holding it in is too painful. The world begins to organize itself around what was taken from us, what went wrong, what can't be repaired. Again, that's understandable. But it's also constricting. It keeps the light out. It keeps us in a cycle of seeing the enemy, the darkness "out there", as a continual threat to our sense of self.

There's a fine line between being heartbroken and becoming identified with our heartbreak.

Victim consciousness says, "This happened *to me,*" and keeps us frozen in the past. It's a protective shell, one that shields us from further pain, but over time, it traps us inside the story of our suffering.

When we shift from "This happened to me " to "This happened, and I am still here," we begin to reclaim our sense of agency, on how we fit in the complex web of being human.

Every time we choose to open the blinds, make the call, take the walk, or breathe through one more day, we are choosing life over the story of victimhood. That choice, small as it may seem, is a declaration of faith in what's still possible for ourselves. Letting the light in may be the most courageous thing we can do.

Chapter 17

Attachment to Suffering: Letting Go Without Letting Go of Love

Sometimes we hold on to pain because it feels like the last thread connecting us to what, or whom, we've lost. We fear that if we loosen our grip, we'll lose them again. Or lose the meaning. Or somehow betray what mattered most.

But love doesn't live in the suffering. It lives in the remembering.

Healing doesn't dishonor what was. It honors it by allowing memory to inspire life, not limit it.

At the beginning, this idea can feel almost impossible. I know. Because it can seem like letting go of suffering means letting go of love. As if easing the pain means we are "moving on" from who we loved or what we cherished. But letting go doesn't mean erasing or forgetting. It means learning how to carry love without letting pain be the only proof that it existed.

Letting go sounds simple, until it's you who has to do it.

In the early days, it feels impossible. Your mind may understand that it's over, the relationship, the dream, the version of life you thought you'd have, but your heart refuses to catch up. You still reach for what's familiar. You still wake expecting things to return to how they were. Every part of you resists the truth.

Letting go is not a single act. It's a series of small reckonings. The slow realization that you can't fix this, can't reverse it, can't make it make sense. And it sucks … but, that's what moving through grief is all about: learning how to be present in the empty space where something sacred once lived and learn to continue to live again.

We talk about "moving on" as if it's a door you walk through and close behind you. But grief doesn't work that way. Time keeps moving, birthdays come, anniversaries arrive, seasons change. The world continues, whether we are ready or not. And all the while, we carry the loss with us.

Each year marks time in quiet, sometimes jarring ways. Another birthday without them. Another holiday that arrives regardless of how we feel. Another reminder that life is moving forward, even though something essential is missing.

What helps is not forcing ourselves to "get past" the loss, but learning how to hold it differently.

For me, the years may pass since Will's death, but my heart has never forgotten, nor will ever forget, the loss. I don't expect it to. Love doesn't disappear with time; it just changes shape. Grief doesn't vanish either; it becomes something we learn to live alongside.

One of the most important things a grieving person needs is for their grief to be witnessed. Space to talk about the loss. Space to say the name. Space to remember out loud. Because grief grows heavier when it's carried alone.

I think of a close friend who lost her daughter just before Christmas. The season came anyway, lights, gatherings, music, expectations. She shared how disorienting it felt to see the world celebrating while her heart was breaking all over again.

What mattered most to her wasn't advice or attempts to cheer her up. It was the small acknowledgments. A text that said, "I remember." A call that didn't avoid mentioning her daughter. Someone willing to sit with her mixed emotions instead of rushing past them.

Those small gestures mattered more than people realize.

Grief doesn't need solutions. It needs presence. It needs someone willing to stay with it for a moment, rather than change the subject or offer perspective too quickly.

Letting go, over time, doesn't mean leaving behind what mattered. It means allowing the loss to have a place in your life without letting it define every moment. It means continuing forward while still carrying love.

Both can exist at the same time.

And slowly, you may notice moments where things feel a little lighter. You can miss them and still laugh at something stupid. You can carry the grief and still build a life. That's part of being human.

Reflection Questions

Take these questions slowly. There's no right pace.

1. As time passes, where do you notice the world moving forward while your grief remains present?

2. What helps you feel less alone with your loss? Talking, remembering, being asked, being acknowledged?

3. Is there a small way you could offer that kind of presence to yourself, or to someone else, this week?

10 Kind Ways to Support Someone Who Is Grieving

1. **Say their name.**
   Don't be afraid to mention the person or what was lost. It helps to know they're remembered.
2. **Reach out, even if you don't know what to say.**
   "I'm thinking of you" or "I remember today" is more than enough.
3. **Listen without trying to fix it.**
   You don't need answers. Just let them talk, or sit quietly if that's what they need.
4. **Check in after the first few weeks.**
   Support often fades just when grief gets heavier. Staying in touch really matters.
5. **Be patient with their timing.**
   Grief doesn't follow a schedule. There's no right pace and no finish line.
6. **Offer help in simple, specific ways.**
   Instead of "let me know," try:
   "Can I bring dinner this week?" or "Want company for a walk?"
7. **Remember the meaningful dates.**
   Birthdays, anniversaries, holidays, a short message that says "I remember" can mean everything.
8. **Let happy moments happen.**
   If they laugh, that's okay. If they cry right after, that's okay too. Both can exist.
9. **Stay when it feels uncomfortable.**
   Grief can be quiet, messy, or heavy. You don't have to make it better, just stay.
10. **Keep showing up in small ways.**
    Little check-ins, notes, or calls often mean more than big gestures.

5 Things *Not* to Say to Someone Who Is Grieving

1. **“Everything happens for a reason.”**
   Even if you believe this, it rarely helps in the moment. Grief needs compassion, not explanations.

2. **“They’re in a better place.”**
   This can unintentionally dismiss the pain of missing them here, now.

3. **“At least…”**
   “At least they lived a long life.”
   “At least you have other children.”
   Comparisons don’t comfort. They minimize.

4. **“You should be feeling better by now.”**
   Grief doesn’t follow a timeline. There is no “by now.”

5. **“Let me know if you need anything.”**
   It sounds supportive, but it puts the burden back on the person who’s already exhausted. It’s kinder to offer something specific.

Chapter 18

The Hardest Letting Go: Returning My Son to the Water

Three years after my son Will passed, during the height of COVID, I decided to take a road trip across America. I didn't know exactly where I was headed: only that I would hike every day in honor of him. I highlighted an old atlas, marking mountain ranges, waterfalls, and wilderness trails that called to me. I wanted to grieve through the land itself, to let the wind, the rocks, and the rivers hold what my heart could not.

For three years, I had kept Will's ashes with me. I told myself it wasn't time yet. But during a conversation with a shamanic healer, she looked at me, almost exasperated, and said, "You need to put his ashes back in the water! How would you like it if you were just held in a box in a closet?"

Her words pierced me. I laughed through tears and said, "I wouldn't."

Because my family was still fractured, I decided to make this ritual my own: a sacred act between a mother, her son, and God.

I drove to the Bearcamp River in the White Mountains of New Hampshire, near the place where Will, as his friends described it, "decided to ascend on his own accord." It was crisp and clear that October morning, sunlight pouring through the trees like a benediction.

I stood by the river's edge, box in my hands, my stomach heavy with dread and love. I lit incense, the smoke curling up like a prayer, and placed the box on the rocky shore. The tears came in waves: the kind that tear you apart and hold you together at once. I felt tortured inside.

I talked to Will. I talked to God. And then, stepping into the cold mountain water, I opened the box. Kneeling, I let the ashes flow from my hands, rebirthing my beautiful son. I watched the current carry him downstream, back into the rhythm of the living world. I cried hard and painful tears. Even writing this, my eyes are filling up with this heart-wrenching yet necessary moment. I am not going to lie, this moment sucked more than anything I have had to bear.

When I burned the box, the smoke rose and merged with the wind, and something in me released. The heaviness didn't disappear, but it changed shape. I felt exhausted, dejected. As I looked up, my eyes settled on a large crucifix spray-painted on an abandoned granite bridge foundation. My heart, heavy with grief, felt the irony as I continued to weep. Grace, it met me right here, ankle deep in the Bear Camp River.

A knowing settled in my heart, and I knew that as hard as it was, I had done the right thing. For Will. And for God.

I whispered to myself, "Kate, you have done it. You birthed an angel, and now you've released that same angel back to God."

That act, both shattering and sacred, marked the beginning of my acceptance of my grief. It wasn't about letting go of Will. It was about returning him to the flow of life, trusting that love, like water, always finds its way home.

And maybe that's what every loss asks of us.

To take what's no longer ours to hold: a person, a dream, a role, a version of ourselves, and release it back to the current of life, trusting that what is meant to remain will always find its way back in another form.

We all have our own ways of finding meaning through loss.

That day, on the banks of the Bearcamp River, I began to find mine.

Reflection Questions

1. What loss are you learning to live with right now? (It might be a person, a dream, a relationship, your health, or a sense of purpose.)

2. Where are you still holding on out of fear and what would it feel like to release that, even a little?

3. How can you honor what's gone by the way you live, love, or show up for others now?

4. When you think of what you've lost, what memory or lesson brings both ache and warmth? That duality: that's grace at work.

5. Write a note of gratitude, not for the ending, but for what was given. Let your tears be part of the ink.

The work of grief is not to let go of love: it's to let love keep growing, even after loss. And grace swoops in as the quiet current that carries us when we no longer know how to swim.

Chapter 19

God, Grace, and Grief

There are moments in life that rearrange your faith forever.

For me, one of those moments came long before I lost my son, Will. He was twenty and carried that kind of presence that made people stop and listen: thoughtful, searching, wise beyond his years. One afternoon, he came to me quietly and said,
"Mom, I think I want to be a monk."

I blinked, half wondering if he was joking.

I was raised Catholic: to have a priest in the family would have been a high honor. But a monk? In a Buddhist monastery? That wasn't something I'd ever imagined for my son.

Then again, holy is holy.

That night, we sat at the kitchen table, opened up Google Earth, searching monasteries across the world. When the map zoomed in on one in Northern California: Abhayagiri, a Thai monastery known as *the home of the smiling monks*, I could feel something sacred in the air. It was like the map was pointing us to something bigger than either of us could name. Will leaned in close to the screen, eyes full of curiosity and peace, and said, "That's it."

I didn't know it then, but God was already preparing me, not for the path I wanted, but for the one I would be asked to walk.

The Wrestling

When Will "ascended on his own accord," as his friends describe it, everything in me shattered. I didn't just lose my son; I lost my sense of order, my certainty, my map of who God was.

There's something about deep loss that pulls the rug out from under every spiritual idea you've ever held. You find yourself asking, *If God is love, then why this?*

People talk about losing faith after tragedy, but what I've learned is that faith doesn't really disappear: it transforms. Sometimes it collapses so that something more honest can be built in its place.

I had to wrestle with the God I thought I knew and make room for the mystery I couldn't understand. I couldn't pray the way I used to; I didn't have the words. My prayers became tears, long walks, whispers of *help*, and moments of quiet surrender.

Therapy helped. But I knew the healing I needed had to be more than psychological; it had to be spiritual. I needed to figure out how to trust God *in* the mess, not after it was cleaned up.

And slowly, grace began to find me, not as comfort or clarity, but as God's presence. A steadying force in the silence. A love that didn't demand answers. A whisper saying, *I'm here, even now.*

Faith in the Fire

People often assume that faith means peace: a soft light that makes everything feel okay. But the truth is, sometimes faith feels like standing in the fire with your arms open, saying, "I don't understand any of this, but I refuse to turn away."

Faith after loss isn't neat. It's gritty, tender, and full of contradictions. Some days, you believe fiercely. Other days, you can barely say God's name. And yet, both days are holy.

I've learned that faith is not about certainty. It's about courage: the courage to stay open when everything in you wants to shut down, to run far, far away.

A New Friend, A Shared Prayer

Not long ago, a woman reached out to me after seeing something I'd shared on social media about Will. She said, "I've been following your posts, and I don't know how you do it, how you talk about your loss with such peace and honesty."

We spoke on the phone, and she told me about her daughter, in her thirties, with two young kids, who was dying of stage four brain cancer. Her voice cracked when she said, "I believe in God, but I'm afraid to bring it up with her. I don't want to upset her."

I could feel her heartbreak through the phone.

So we practiced.
I said, "Let's just start here. Let's pray together."

We prayed for her daughter by name, bringing her into the circle of our conversation, not as a medical case, but as a sacred life, still shining. I asked God to meet them both in their fear and in their love.

Afterward, she whispered, "I didn't realize how much I needed that."

These are the moments that matter most to me.

Not the polished ones. Not the public ones.
The quiet, often unseen moments that actually change people.

Meeting someone exactly where they are.
Asking the questions that are hard and necessary.
Holding space where grief and grace can exist at the same time.

We live in a culture that barely knows how to talk about grief.
It's acknowledged in whispers, in awkward pauses, in conversations that happen *around* the person who is hurting instead of with them.

I'm committed to changing that. To have more honest, open conversations about grief and other feelings we are afraid to name: about who we are in it, and who we become because of it. The lessons it teaches us. The love that remains. The way loss reshapes us without defining us.

That's what spiritual ministry looks like to me.

Not preaching to people, but sitting beside them.
Not having the right words, but being willing to stay.
Praying when someone can't find the words themselves.
And gently reminding them, again and again, that love hasn't gone anywhere.

To the Reader Who Isn't Sure About God

Maybe you're reading this, and you're not sure what you believe. Maybe you've lost someone and the word "God" feels too loaded, or maybe you've decided that faith just isn't for you.
That's okay.

This isn't about converting you, it's about comforting you. It's about reminding you that mystery is big enough to hold your doubt, your anger, your silence. You don't need a label or a creed to experience grace.

Call it love, life, energy, presence, something beyond us that somehow holds us together when we fall apart. I've seen it too many times to dismiss it.

You don't have to understand it. You just have to stay open to the possibility that, even in the darkness, something sacred is still reaching for you.

Kate McKay

The Mystery and the Mercy

I used to think faith was something you mastered, that the goal was certainty. Now I think the holiest thing we can do is surrender to mystery.

I still don't have all the answers. I never will. But I know this: God isn't just in the light. God is also in the darkness, in the broken, the raw, the human.

And sometimes, the most sacred prayer is simply staying open long enough to notice that grace is still flickering even through our suffering.

Reflection: The Sacred Work of Wrestling with Faith

Grief changes not only what we feel, but what we believe. It can dismantle the old ways we've understood God, love, and ourselves, and that's part of the sacred work. These questions aren't meant to give you answers, but to help you listen more deeply to your own experience.

1. When you think about your loss, what happens to your understanding of God: does it expand, contract, or change shape altogether?

2. Where have you experienced moments of grace, even fleeting ones, since your loss?
   Who or what helped you feel less alone, even for a breath?

3. What version of faith or hope no longer fits who you are today? What are you being invited to release so something truer can take its place?

4. If you could speak honestly to God, the Universe, or Love itself, what would you say?

5. Who are the "smiling monks" in your life right now, the people or places that remind you that peace still exists?
   (How might you let them in, even a little more?)

6. When you think about your loved one, what feels eternal, what love, lesson, or presence still lives on through you? (Let this remembrance be a form of prayer.)

7. What does grace mean to you now? *How might it look or sound in the* middle of your grief, not as a fix, but as a companion?

8. If faith could hold both your doubt and your devotion, what would that faith look like?

   (Can you imagine a relationship with the divine that welcomes every emotion, even your anger and silence?)

Q&A: When Faith Feels Far Away

1. How could God let this happen?

That's the question, isn't it?

The one we whisper when no one's listening and shout when the pain gets too loud.

If God is love, how could this happen?

There isn't a clean answer, and maybe that's the point. Grief doesn't mean God has abandoned us; it means we're standing in the middle of mystery. Love doesn't erase loss. Faith doesn't guarantee protection. But somewhere in the wreckage, if we stay open, grace still flickers.

I don't believe God lets tragedy happen as a punishment or lesson. I believe God enters it, right into the mess, into the ache, into the ordinary moments when we can't take one more thing. Not as a judge or a puppeteer, but as Presence itself, aching with us, breathing with us, holding what we can't hold alone.

Sometimes that's all faith is after loss, not certainty, but the faint whisper: I'm not alone, even in this.

2. I used to have such strong faith. I feel like it's been shattered.

You're not broken. You're growing.

When everything in life collapses, your beliefs often have to collapse too. The version of faith that once held you may not be wide enough for the pain you've seen. That doesn't mean you've lost faith;it means your faith is being remade.

There's a kind of faith that thrives when life is easy, and then there's the faith that rises from the ashes. It's quieter, humbler, more real. It doesn't say, "Everything happens for a reason." It says, "Even this can be met with love."

That's resurrection faith, not shiny or loud, but forged in the fire.

3. I wasn't brought up in faith, but through my loss, I've deepened it. Now people think I'm a 'Jesus lover' and have ostracized me.

Welcome to the paradox of grace.

When you start healing through faith, not everyone will understand. Some will be curious, others uncomfortable. People love the version of us they can predict, and when grief awakens something sacred in us, when we begin to seek God, it unsettles the balance.

Your story is sacred, even if others don't "get it." Faith that grows out of heartbreak is the most authentic kind; it's not borrowed, inherited, or trendy. It's forged in tears and truth. So if your path with God has made others pull away, let that distance be your teacher, not your shame.

Faith doesn't require approval. It requires honesty.

You're not here to prove your belief; you're here to live it, in love, in grace, in your own authentic way.

4. How do I pray when I feel like a mess?

Start messy. God's not afraid of your chaos.

Prayer isn't a performance. It's conversation … and sometimes confrontation. There are days when my prayers sound more like arguments than hymns. And that's okay. God doesn't need polished words; God wants presence.

Prayer can look like sitting in silence, walking in nature, listening to music, journaling, crying in the car, whispering "help," or saying nothing at all.

It's not always rainbows and sprinkles, sometimes it's like the World Wide Wrestling League. But even in that battle, your soul moves. You move. And that movement is grace.

For me, prayer has become less about talking and more about being. Sometimes I just breathe and imagine God breathing with me. Other times, I pray with my feet, walking, running, showing up for life even when my heart is tired.

There is no wrong way to pray. The fact that you're reaching, that you're still open enough to ask, "How?" that is prayer.

5. Does doubt mean I've lost my faith?

No. Doubt is not the opposite of faith; it's part of it.

Every relationship that matters involves questioning, even with God. Doubt is the crack where honesty gets in. It's what keeps faith alive and evolving. If we can't question God, then what kind of love is that?

The holiest prayers I've ever prayed began with doubt.

"Where are You?"

"Why me?"

"Are You still there?"

And somehow, through the asking, something opened. Doubt is not the death of belief; it's the doorway to a deeper one.

Scripture to Reflect On

Here are a few verses you might include. Each offers a slightly different energy, depending on how you want to end the section:

- Psalm 34:18 "The Lord is close to the brokenhearted and saves those who are crushed in spirit."
- Isaiah 43:2 "When you pass through the waters, I will be with you; and through the rivers, they shall not overwhelm you."
- Romans 8:26 "The Spirit helps us in our weakness … the Spirit himself intercedes for us through wordless groans."
- Psalm 46:10 "Be still, and know that I am God."
- 2 Corinthians 12:9 "My grace is sufficient for you, for my power is made perfect in weakness."

Closing Reflection

Faith after loss isn't about having answers. It's about daring to stay open: to mystery, to grace, to life itself. It's about learning to meet both your pain and your peace with reverence.

Whether you call it God, Love, or simply Presence, something holy still meets you here.
Even in your doubt, even in your wrestling, you are not alone. And that, that flicker of connection, is where grace begins again.

Chapter 20

Meaning Rising:
Finding Your Way After Loss

After a loss, it can feel like the internal hard drive has been wiped clean. Who you were. What defined you as a human being. What you cared about. Gone.

What's left isn't some wild new insights; it's brain fog. Confusion. Disrupted sleep. Irritation you can't quite explain. An emptiness that settles in, along with a future that feels undefined and strangely uninteresting. Even imagining what *could* be feels like too much effort.

Sometimes that state lasts days. Sometimes weeks. Sometimes years.

And much to our disappointment, meaning does not come back like a lightning bolt from Zeus, no thunder, no divine explanation, no sudden clarity. Nope, it sure doesn't.

Instead, meaning returns in small ways, as life slowly begins to reassemble itself. Not cleanly. Not completely. More like a puzzle with missing pieces you can't find under the couch cushions, the dining room table, or anywhere else you think to look.

What does return is something quieter: a mustard seed of hope. The faintest suggestion that there may still be more: more life, more purpose, more meaning, and one day, a brand-new puzzle appears, awaiting your assembly.

Letting Go of the Why to Live What's Next

Most losses don't make logical sense. No explanation ties things up neatly or makes the pain feel justified. But we sure do try, don't we? I know I have stewed for hours trying to figure my grief out.

And it's so easy to get stuck in the *why*. The mind wants details. The ego wants the reason, something it can analyze, blame, and control in order to feel some semblance of sense in what is often a nonsensical loss. If we can understand it, maybe it won't hurt as much, we believe with our whole heart.

But often, the most courageous thing we can do is let go of the *why*. Not because it doesn't matter, but because it can keep us trapped, circling questions that will never give us what we're actually longing for: some sense of relief, of peace.

What requires even more courage is sitting with the more difficult question: *What now?*

And the good news? When we open our hearts to the *"What now?"* grace shows up right there. Not with answers or explanations, but as permission: to stop forcing meaning, to stop demanding closure, to take the next small step without having the whole picture.

Grace doesn't rush the healing. It meets us in the uncertainty and reminds us that moving forward without answers is not failure, it's faith in motion. And as a reminder that it is due time, to let the love back in.

A Client's Story: From Surviving to Living

My client Paul, who once carried so much guilt, eventually told me something I'll never forget.

He said, "I stopped trying to get back to who I was. I realized he's gone. But who I am now, I actually like him, understand him. He's actually pretty awesome."

That's the heart of meaning rising.

It's when you start to live from what loss has taught you, instead of what it took from you. You begin to get to know the person you are now, and with the help of grace, learn to honor the new version of you.

In the coming months, Paul began mentoring younger men in his community, showing up for them in ways he wished someone had for him. He found fulfillment, not because his pain was gone, but because it had been repurposed into serving others.

That's the alchemy of meaning: when what broke you becomes what turns out helping to build others.

The Reorientation of the Heart

After a profound loss, your compass changes. What once mattered, (recognition, perfection, approval), starts to lose its hold. And what remains are the things that can't be bought or faked: truth, time, presence, love.

Meaning isn't about arriving somewhere new; it's about recognizing that you've been transformed into a new version of you. It's when you realize you can hold both grief and gratitude in the same breath and feel no contradiction between them.

That's the magic of grace.

Living the Legacy of Love

Whatever or whoever you've lost, the love remains. That's what meaning ultimately is: a way to keep love alive through action, intention, and presence. Love doesn't end; it evolves. It flows through the way you live now, how you show up for others, how you honor yourself, how you create, give, forgive, and keep moving forward.

When you live with that awareness, life itself becomes sacred again. Not perfect. Not pain-free. But sacred, precisely because it's fragile and fleeting and still so worth showing up for.

Reflection Questions

1. How has your loss changed what you value or how you show up in the world?

2. Where are you already living your meaning in your work, your relationships, your creativity, your faith?

3. What would it look like to turn one lesson from your grief into something that serves or uplifts someone else?

Chapter 21

Living Forward

And eventually, the landscape of grief begins to look different. The ache is still there, but it softens around the edges. You start to see small flashes of light, moments of quiet peace, laughter, or simple gratitude that surprise you.

This isn't forgetting. It's the slow work of *acceptance.*

Acceptance doesn't mean you stop missing who or what you've lost. Not at all. It means you begin to let life reach for you again. You start to believe that joy and sorrow can exist in the same breath, that hope can live beside heartbreak.

Living forward isn't about moving on. It's about *moving with.* It's taking the love, the lessons, and even the pain, and weaving them into the way you live now. It's letting faith and purpose start to reveal themselves again, not as hard and fast answers, but as companions on the undefined path ahead.

Living forward means acknowledging that even with all that's been lost, life still calls to you, quietly, persistently, toward connection, meaning, even, dare we say it, a sense of renewal.

The Slow Return to Life

At first, living forward can feel disorienting. You may catch yourself laughing and feel guilty.
You may find joy and wonder if you're allowed to. You may step into something new and feel the shadow of what's gone hovering nearby.

That's all part of it.

Healing doesn't mean you stop missing; it means your heart learns to hold absence and presence in the same space.

Creating from What Remains

Grief often strips us bare. But what's left after everything else falls away is the most honest version of you. This is where meaning begins to take form, not as a grand revelation, but as small, daily acts of courage.

Maybe it's writing, painting, cooking, planting something new, or volunteering where compassion is needed. Maybe it's saying yes to opportunities that once felt too big, or too late. Maybe it's simply deciding to love again, in any way that love can still be expressed.

Please understand this important thing: Living forward isn't graceful or certain. It's messy, uneven, and full of days you don't know how you'll do it. But you do. You will. One breath, one choice, one act of courage at a time.

A Client's Story: Mark- Life Reimagined

One of my clients, Mark, came to me after losing his business, a venture that had defined his identity for decades. He wasn't grieving death, but he was grieving who he thought he was.

He said, "I don't even know where to start."

So we began with one question: *What still feels alive in you?*

At first, his answers were small, cooking for his kids, hiking, and the satisfaction of fixing things with his hands. But slowly, those small actions began to seed something new in him.

Mark started mentoring young entrepreneurs, helping them avoid the same pitfalls he had faced. His loss didn't disappear, but it transformed into purpose. That's the essence of living forward, turning pain into presence, memory into meaning.

There's no single *"after"* in grief. There's only the next breath, the next step, the next moment when you say yes to life, even when your heart is still broken. Grace becomes your rhythm.

It's how you move now, not perfectly, but consciously. Some days it's easier. Some days it's more difficult. Some days it's just enough to whisper, *I'm still here.*

Choosing How to Live

When you live forward, you begin to ask different questions:

1. How can I make what I've lived through matter?
2. How can I carry love, not pain, as my compass?
3. What can I create, give, or become from all I've learned?

This is how love keeps expanding: through the choices you make, the lives you touch, the light you allow back in.

You will never forget what you've lost. At times and sometimes, more often than you care to even admit, the grief will swoop in and feel like a punch in the gut. You find yourself catching your breath. A tear, a frozen moment.

But you will find new ways to honor what you lost, through kindness, courage, honesty, and the grace to keep growing. That's what living forward means. It's not the end of your grief. It's the continuation of your love.

Reflection Questions

1. What small ways can you begin to say "yes" to life again?

2. How might you turn part of your pain into something that serves or uplifts others?

3. What new rhythm of grace do you want to live by?

Living forward isn't about erasing the past. It's about bringing its love into your present, one brave step at a time.

Epilogue

What Remains

Grief doesn't follow a timeline.
Some days you'll feel like you're moving forward, and the next, you'll wonder if you've made any progress at all.
There will be moments when you feel steady, and others when the sadness hits like it just happened yesterday.
That's not failure, that's real life after loss.

It's messy. It's uncomfortable. It's confusing.
Sometimes it feels like you're walking through fog with no sense of direction, just putting one foot in front of the other because stopping isn't an option.
And that's okay.

Healing isn't about arriving somewhere peaceful; it's about learning how to live inside the unrest.
You may still feel anger, guilt, exhaustion, or loneliness. You may even feel frustrated that you're still feeling anything at all.
But the truth is, you're doing exactly what grief asks of you: showing up, however imperfectly, with what's real.

Please don't try to carry it all alone.
You don't have to be strong every day.
You don't have to know what comes next.
You just have to stay open; open to love, to help, to being seen.

Reach out.
Find your people, the ones who can sit with you in the silence without trying to fix it.
Let yourself be cared for, even when it feels easier to retreat.
You deserve to be witnessed, held, and reminded that your story still matters.

If this book has done anything, I hope it's reminded you that you're not alone. That your grief is not too much, and your healing doesn't have to be perfect. That grace isn't found in pretending you're okay: it's found in allowing yourself to be human.

Keep going, one breath at a time.
Keep choosing to love, even when it hurts.
Keep saying yes to life, even when it feels uncertain.

Because this is what remains:
Love that keeps finding its way through the cracks.
Grace that keeps showing up when you least expect it.
And life, still calling you forward, one brave step at a time.

I'm here with you.
You are not alone.
Stay connected.
Keep your heart open.
Let others care for you as you learn to live again.

That, my friend, is how love continues.

A Final Reflection

1. What qualities did you most love in who or what you lost, and how might you embody them now?

2. Where in your life can you bring more of that love, patience, humor, or courage into the world?

3. How might grief become not just something to survive, but something that teaches you how to live more fully?

Your heart may always carry the imprint of what you've lost. But it will also carry the light of what remains, love that refuses to end, grace that never stops rising.

Resources for Your Healing Journey

Grief takes many forms: death, divorce, illness, identity shifts, betrayal, the loss of a dream, or even a future we imagined.

Whatever loss you're carrying, please remember: you don't have to walk through it alone.

The following national organizations and programs offer comfort, tools, and connection for people navigating all kinds of grief and transition.

Grief & Bereavement Support

The Compassionate Friends (TCF)

For families grieving the death of a child, sibling, or grandchild of any age and from any cause.

Website: compassionatefriends.org

Phone: 877-969-0010

GriefShare

A 13-week support program for anyone mourning the death of a loved one. Sessions are held both in person and online.

Website: griefshare.org

Stephen Ministries

Christian-based, one-on-one confidential care for those walking through loss or life challenges.

Website: stephenministries.org

Grief.com David Kessler

Founded by grief expert David Kessler, Grief.com offers compassionate education, online support, and courses for all kinds of loss. Kessler is known for introducing the sixth stage of grief — finding meaning.

Website: grief.com

American Foundation for Suicide Prevention (AFSP)

Resources, community, and healing programs for those impacted by suicide loss.

Website: afsp.org

TAPS Tragedy Assistance Program for Survivors

Comfort, care, and connection for those grieving the death of a military loved one.

Website: taps.org

SAVE Suicide Awareness Voices of Education

For survivors of suicide loss and those supporting them.

Website: save.org

Relationship & Life Transition Support

DivorceCare

Support groups for those navigating the pain of separation or divorce.

Website: divorcecare.or

Al-Anon Family Groups

Support for families and friends affected by a loved one's drinking or addiction.

Website: al-anon.org

SMART Recovery Family & Friends

Evidence-based support for those affected by someone else's addictive behaviors.

Website: smartrecovery.org/family

Cancer Support Community

Resources and groups for individuals and families navigating cancer and anticipatory grief.

Website: cancersupportcommunity.org

AARP Caregiving & Grief Resources

Guidance for those caring for aging loved ones or facing the transition after caregiving ends.

Website: aarp.org/caregiving/grief-los

Rainbow Bridge Pet Loss Grief Center

A comforting online space for anyone mourning the loss of a beloved animal companion.

Website: rainbowsbridge.com/griefsupportcenter

Trauma, Identity & Spiritual Growth Resources

RAINN (Rape, Abuse & Incest National Network)

24/7 support for survivors of sexual trauma or abuse — grief can include the loss of safety or identity.

Website: rainn.org

Hotline: 800-656-HOPE (4673)

The Center for Loss & Life Transition

Founded by Dr. Alan Wolfelt, this center offers workshops and writings on the art of companioning through grief.

Website: centerforloss.com

Spiritual Directors International (SDI)

A global network connecting people seeking spiritual guidance or accompaniment through major life changes.

Website: sdiworld.org

National Alliance on Mental Illness (NAMI)

Education, peer support, and advocacy for those navigating mental illness or loss of mental health stability.

Website: nami.org

Helpline: 800-950-NAMI (6264)

For Further Reading and Reflection

Books that have offered wisdom, language, and companionship on the road through grief.

Grief is not a journey meant to be traveled alone.
The words of others: their stories, science, prayers, and hard-won insights can help us find meaning when our own feels lost. These are some of the books that have spoken truth to me and to the many people I've coached and sat beside as a spiritual director and grief educator.

Each of these voices has, in its own way, reminded me that healing is less about moving on and more about learning how to live and love again. I offer them to you with gratitude and the hope that one or more will whisper exactly what you need to hear.

On Grief, Loss, and Healing

- **On Grief and Grieving** *Elisabeth Kübler-Ross & David Kessler*
  A foundational guide through the stages of grief, illuminating how love and loss are intertwined.

- **Finding Meaning: The Sixth Stage of Grief** *David Kessler*
  A powerful continuation of Kübler-Ross's work, exploring how we can make meaning from pain.

- **It's OK That You're Not OK** *Megan Devine*
  A deeply validating read that rejects clichés and honors grief as a love story, not a problem to solve.

- **Bearing the Unbearable** *Joanne Cacciatore*
  A profoundly compassionate book that blends mindfulness, ritual, and psychology to accompany those in deep sorrow.

- **The Wild Edge of Sorrow** *Francis Weller*
  A poetic and soulful reflection on grief as an initiation — a path toward deeper connection with self, community, and the sacred.

The Body and Emotional Healing

- **The Body Keeps the Score** *Bessel van der Kolk, M.D.*
  Groundbreaking research on how trauma and grief live in the body — and how healing happens through reconnection.

- **Emotional Agility** *Susan David, Ph.D.*
  A compassionate guide to understanding our emotions and cultivating flexibility and presence through them.

- **Resilient** *Rick Hanson, Ph.D.*
  Neuroscience meets compassion: how to grow calm, strength, and happiness through the practice of inner safety.

- **Moving Through Grief** *Gretchen Schmelzer*
  A practical and tender look at how movement, breath, and ritual can help us process loss physically.

Spiritual Growth and Grace

- **When Everything Falls Apart** *Pema Chödrön*
  Timeless wisdom on staying open, kind, and awake in the midst of pain.

- **A Grace Disguised: How the Soul Grows Through Loss** *Jerry Sittser*
  A luminous exploration of how suffering can enlarge the soul without erasing the ache.

- **Learning to Walk in the Dark** *Barbara Brown Taylor*
  A powerful invitation to trust the sacred work that happens in seasons of darkness.

- **The Return of the Prodigal Son** *Henri Nouwen*
  A moving meditation on forgiveness, belonging, and homecoming through one of Jesus's most beloved parables.

- **The Inner Voice of Love** *Henri Nouwen*
  Nouwen's private journal from a season of despair: raw, tender, and deeply human.

Resilience, Purpose, and Meaning-Making

- **Man's Search for Meaning** *Viktor E. Frankl*
  The classic testament to human strength and purpose, even in the darkest conditions.

- **The Choice** *Dr. Edith Eva Eger*
  A memoir of survival and healing that reveals how freedom begins in the mind and the heart.

- **Option B** *Sheryl Sandberg & Adam Grant*
  An accessible and heartfelt exploration of resilience and rebuilding joy after loss.

- **Untamed** *Glennon Doyle*
  A bold reminder that loss of identity can become a gateway to truth, freedom, and authenticity.

- **Everything Happens for a Reason (and Other Lies I've Loved)** *Kate Bowler*
  A beautifully written reflection on faith, illness, and finding grace without needing easy answers.

For Companions, Caregivers, and Friends

- **How to Carry What Can't Be Fixed** *Megan Devine*
  A companion journal full of gentle prompts for those living with ongoing loss.

- **Don't Sing Songs to a Heavy Heart** *Kenneth C. Haugk*
  Practical and compassionate guidance for those supporting the bereaved.

- **Healing After Loss** *Martha Whitmore Hickman*
  A classic daily meditation offering comfort, faith, and grounding wisdom one page at a time.

A Note for Your Journey

Whatever loss you carry: a person, a dream, a role, a relationship, a version of yourself, please remember:

Your pain is real. Your timeline is your own. And you are not alone.

Reach out. Connect. Speak your story.

Every time you do, you invite grace into the room.

Healing doesn't mean forgetting: It means allowing love to find new ways to live through you.

May these resources remind you that help exists, hope remains, and love never dies.

Q & A: When Grief Feels Too Big

These are some of the questions I've been asked, and the ones I've lived myself.

There aren't perfect answers, only honest ones. What matters is that you keep showing up, even when your heart feels like it's breaking open.

Q: How do I release this rage that I feel?

A: Rage is grief in motion.

It's the body's way of saying, This mattered.

Don't try to bury it. Give it somewhere to go- move, cry, walk, write, lift, scream in the car. Find a grief support group. Hire a therapist or grief coach. Rage is sacred energy when you let it flow safely.

When you stop judging it, it starts to transform.

And underneath the anger, if you listen closely, there's often love- fierce, protective, still reaching for what was lost.

Q: I can't stop crying. What do I do?

A: Crying is not a sign of weakness. It's release.

Tears are your body's language when words can't reach that far.

Let them come. Don't apologize for them. Drink water, rest, breathe.

When the tears come in waves, imagine they're carrying you closer to shore, not away from it.

You're not breaking down, you're breaking open.

Q: People keep telling me it's been a year, that it's time to move on. Why can't I?

A: Because grief doesn't own a clock.

It moves like the tide, unpredictable, stubborn, sacred.

Those who haven't walked your path may not understand that grief isn't something you get over; it's something you grow around.

You're not behind. You're human.

Let your timeline be your own.

Q: How can I talk about my grief in a way that's affirming, not depressing?

A: Affirming grief starts with truth.

You can speak from pain and from perspective at the same time.

Try:

- "I'm learning to live with this, one day at a time."
- "I still miss them, but I'm finding new ways to keep love alive."
- "This changed me, and I'm still here."

Grief is not a failure of strength; it's a reflection of love. The right people won't flinch when you tell the truth.

Q: What are the ways I can practice self-care through grief?

A: Keep it simple and kind.

- Rest. Grief is work.
- Move. Let your body release what your heart can't name.
- Nourish. Eat, hydrate, take your vitamins — it's not vanity, it's stability.
- Connect. Be with those who allow silence and tears.
- Create. Write, draw, garden, pray — anything that lets you express what words can't.
- Remember. Speak their name. Keep their memory present.

You're not rebuilding; you're re-connection to who you are in a new way.

Q: I've lost a relationship(s) through my grief. Everything feels different. Some people have drifted away, while others have shown up. How do I handle that?

A: Grief rearranges your relationships.

It reveals who can meet you in the deep end, and who can't. I get it. This part really sucks.

Try not to see the ones who fall away as rejection. Think of it as a revelation.

You're evolving, and your connections will, too.

Honor what was, bless what is, and make room for what's next.

The right people will meet you where you are, not where you used to be.

Q: I feel so much guilt. How did I not know?

A: Guilt is part of the grief-guilt bridge; it's what our minds do when our hearts can't comprehend the loss.

We replay, rewrite, and punish ourselves because doing so feels like a way to stay connected.

But guilt isn't truth. It's love, tangled in self-blame.

You did the best you could with what you knew at the time.

Forgiveness, especially of yourself, doesn't mean forgetting. It means allowing your love to exist without punishment.

Q: What are ways I can honor my loss?

A: Honoring doesn't mean living in the past; it means carrying love forward.

Think about what you most loved in who or what you lost- their humor, patience, kindness, curiosity, strength. Then, choose to embody those qualities in your daily life.

That's how love keeps breathing through you.

Create rituals: light a candle, visit a favorite place, write them a letter, or start a new tradition in their name.

You don't have to "move on." You can move with, through, and alongside your grief, through remembrance, action, and meaning.

Q: How can I talk about grief with others?

A: Gently, honestly, and without apology.

You can say, "I'm not looking for advice, I just need you to listen," or, "I'm having a hard day and could use some company."

Not everyone will know how to respond- that's okay.

Your honesty gives others permission to be more human, too.

And sometimes, your openness helps someone else begin their own healing.

Q: How can I support someone who's grieving?

A: Show up. Stay. Repeat.

Don't worry about the perfect thing to say, say something or say nothing. Either is ok. Your presence is what matters.

"I'm here." "You don't have to go through this alone." "I can sit with you."

Bring meals. Send small texts weeks or months later- that's when grief often deepens.

Remember important dates. Ask about the person they lost.

Let them cry, or laugh, or be silent.

Presence heals more than words ever can.

Final Thoughts

Grief is proof of love.

And love, when tended to, will always find new ways to grow.

When you start embodying the qualities of who or what you've lost, you become a living continuation of that love.

That's how grace moves, through you, through us, through every act of compassion that keeps love alive.

You don't have to rush.

Just keep breathing, keep noticing, keep swimming.

Meaning is already rising.

Conclusion

The Sacred Dance of Grief and Grace

Grief will change you. There's no way around that.

But grace- grace will change and deepen the ways you heal and find meaning through the mess, You won't be the same person you were before loss.

You'll be deeper, wiser, more awake to what matters. You'll notice beauty in ordinary things, tenderness in strangers, and the quiet power of simply being here, breathing, alive.

At first, you may think you're walking through the valley of sorrow alone. But somewhere along the way, grace begins to walk beside you- in the laughter that returns without warning, in the sunrise that suddenly feels like a promise, in the hand you extend to someone else still finding their way.

Grief doesn't leave us untouched. It leaves us transformed.

What begins as a fracture becomes the place where the light enters.

And what feels like an ending becomes an initiation- into deeper empathy, fiercer love, and a strength that no storm can take.

The Continuing Bond

There will always be moments when it hits fresh, a date, a scent, a song that stirs what once was.
But now, instead of collapsing under it, you breathe through it.

The grief is no longer a wound; it's a living reminder of how deeply you've loved.

And here's the grace: every time you embody what you loved most, their kindness, humor, courage, curiosity, or compassion, you bring that love back into the world.

When you act with their generosity, when you laugh the way they laughed, when you show up the way they would have shown up, you keep them alive in you.

That's not just remembrance. It's resurrection.

It's how we honor the people, the seasons, and the dreams we've lost, by carrying forward the qualities that made them matter.
Grief may change your world, but it can also change your way of loving.

What Remains

Grief doesn't follow a timeline.
Some days you'll feel like you're moving forward, and the next, you'll wonder if you've made any progress at all.
There will be moments when you feel steady, and others when the sadness hits like it just happened yesterday.
That's not failure, that's real life after loss.

It's messy. It's uncomfortable. It's confusing.
Sometimes it feels like you're walking through fog with no sense of direction, just putting one foot in front of the other because stopping isn't an option.
And that's okay.

Healing isn't about arriving somewhere peaceful; it's about learning how to live inside the unrest.
You may still feel anger, guilt, exhaustion, or loneliness. You may even feel frustrated that you're still feeling anything at all.
But the truth is, you're doing exactly what grief asks of you showing up, however imperfectly, with what's real.

Please don't try to carry it all alone.
You don't have to be strong every day.
You don't have to know what comes next.
You just have to stay open, open to love, to help, to being seen.

Reach out.
Find your people, the ones who can sit with you in the silence without trying to fix it.
Let yourself be cared for, even when it feels easier to retreat.
You deserve to be witnessed, held, and reminded that your story still matters.

If this book has done anything, I hope it's reminded you that you're not alone.
That your grief is not too much, and your healing doesn't have to be perfect.
That grace isn't found in pretending you're okay, it's found in allowing yourself to be human.

Keep going, one breath at a time.
Keep choosing to love, even when it hurts.
Keep saying yes to life, even when it feels uncertain.

Because this is what remains:
Love that keeps finding its way through the cracks.
Grace that keeps showing up when you least expect it.
And life, still calling you forward, one brave step at a time.

I'm here with you.
You are not alone.
Stay connected.
Keep your heart open.
Let others care for you as you learn to live again.

That, my friend, is how love continues.

This was the book I needed, the one I couldn't find when my own world fell apart.
If these words have met you where you are, I hope they've reminded you that healing isn't a straight line and that love never really leaves.
I would love to hear from you, your story, your questions, what you're learning as you live forward.

Join me in the conversation on **Facebook at @GriefandGrace** and if you're looking for deeper support, you can schedule a **Discovery Call** to explore how we might work together — whether that's one-on-one coaching, group work, or having me speak at your organization or event.

You don't have to do this alone.
Keep walking. Keep connecting. Keep letting grace find you, right where you are.

What is a Grief Coach?

If there's one truth I've learned through it all, it's this: healing happens in relationship.

We don't find our way through pain by isolating; we find it by being witnessed, by being held in understanding, by walking together toward meaning.

It's not about "getting over" anything.

It's about allowing the experience of loss to open you to deeper connection, with yourself, with others, with something larger than any one of us.

A Blessing for the Journey

May you learn to hold your sorrow gently, as proof of how deeply you have loved.

May you give yourself permission to feel it all: the ache, the anger, Please attitude, the grace.

May you see that strength and softness are not opposites, but partners.

And may you remember: you are not broken. You are becoming.

Grief and grace are not separate stories.

They are on the same winding path, one side shadowed, the other light-filled.

Keep moving. Keep listening. Keep loving.

Book Your Discovery Call

If these words have met you where you are, know this: your story matters.

You don't have to walk this road alone.

I invite you to take the next step, not into perfection, but into presence.

Join me for a Discovery Call, a compassionate, private conversation where we'll explore what's next for you: how to bring light to your loss, honor your story, and begin transforming pain into purpose.

Book a Discovery Call with Kate: https://calendly.com/katemckay/restorative-coaching

www.ingramcontent.com/pod-product-compliance
Lightning Source LLC
LaVergne TN
LVHW010659110826
845149LV00014B/3157

* 9 7 8 1 9 7 2 0 1 4 0 4 2 *